Bobby Dazzlers

Bobby Dazzlers: My Story as a UK Policewoman in the 70s
Copyright © 2023 by Maureen Coonrod

Published in the United States of America
ISBN   Paperback: 979-8-89091-500-9
ISBN   eBook: 979-8-89091-501-6

All rights reserved. No part of this publication may be reproduced, stored in a retrieval system or transmitted in any way by any means, electronic, mechanical, photocopy, recording or otherwise without the prior permission of the author except as provided by USA copyright law.

The opinions expressed by the author are not necessarily those of ReadersMagnet, LLC.

ReadersMagnet, LLC
10620 Treena Street, Suite 230 | San Diego, California, 92131 USA
1.619. 354. 2643 | www.readersmagnet.com

Book design copyright © 2023 by ReadersMagnet, LLC. All rights reserved.

Cover design by Tifanny Curaza
Interior design by Daniel Lopez

Bobby Dazzlers

My Story as a UK Policewoman in the '70s

MAUREEN COONROD

ReadersMagnet, LLC

TABLE OF CONTENTS

DEDICATION..7
ACKNOWLEDGMENTS..9

CHAPTER ONE..17
CHAPTER TWO 27
CHAPTER THREE..36
CHAPTER FOUR..40
CHAPTER FIVE 58
CHAPTER SIX 68
CHAPTER SEVEN 77
CHAPTER EIGHT 89
CHAPTER NINE...101
CHAPTER TEN 112
CHAPTER ELEVEN 124
CHAPTER TWELVE 145
CHAPTER THIRTEEN 153
CHAPTER FOURTEEN 163
CHAPTER FIFTEEN 177
CHAPTER SIXTEEN 185
CHAPTER SEVENTEEN 189
CHAPTER EIGTHEEN 195
CHAPTER NINETEEN 200

RESEARCH REFERENCES 206
ABOUT THE AUTHOR..207

DEDICATION

To all law enforcement officers in the U.K. and U.S.A. who put their lives on the line everyday, I salute your hardwork and dedicate this book to you.

ACKNOWLEDGMENTS

My inspiration for writing this book was my grandmother, Lilian Emily Jane Hatter, who was born in the 1800's into a world where women were an appendage to men, with no rights to say or do what they really wanted to. Her family were wealthy and their business was safe making, but through a bad unpaid debt to them, the family went bankrupt and went from riches to rags overnight.

The shock killed Lilian's mother, leaving my grandmother, the eldest daughter, to bring up her siblings. She went from having servants to being one, sowing sequins on to her mistresses' gala dresses and shoes.

She suffered hardship and loss. After the First World War was over, Lilian's husband returned sick due to mustard gas poisoning and after he died, she was left to bring up her two children alone. As a child I listened in awe of the life she had and all the stories from living wealthy and poor, no middle class. I wanted to be so much like her, to be capable of loving without expecting anything in return, giving without reward and helping people less fortunate than myself.

I had always wanted to be in the police force and Lilian encouraged me to take the first step. Now it was my turn to tell her of my stories. I thank her for giving me my strength and determination to live my life to the fullest...this one is for you Nan; you will always be in my heart.

Uniforms of the Women Police Service through the ages

History of Women Police Officers in the U.K.

The founders of the Women Police Service in 1914 were a militant suffragette journalist called Nina Boyle and an anti-slavery campaigner called Margaret Damer Dawson.

Boyle took advantage of the First World War by using women in the place of men on the streets to prove that women would be invaluable, and afterwards could be made a permanent part of the police force. Dawson's idea was to organize woman into a group to be used to deter pimps and women from entering into prostitution.

The then Commissioner of Police, Sir Edward Henry, allowed them to patrol the streets, gave them identity cards and gave them the specific job or rescuing prostitutes from their way of life.

Police were given instructions to help them, but they were never actually enlisted to work within the Metropolitan Police. The women renamed themselves as "The Women Police Service" (WPS), as previously they were known as "Volunteers."

They adopted the same ranks as they had in the Metropolitan Police Force which included sergeants and inspectors.

In 1915, Grantham in the North of England was the first rural force that felt the need to help with juveniles and women so Grantham Police Force swore in Mrs Edith Smith, giving her full powers of arrest which made history as now she was the first proper Policewoman in Britain with the same powers as a male officer.

Later in 1915, Lloyd George and Winston Churchill, both successive ministers for munitions, requested that uniformed officer from the WPS in London be put into the munitions factories to "police" the women workers.

> ### British Slang Definitions
> **Dog's bollocks**—awesome
> **Lost the plot**—Gone Crazy
> **Collywobbles** — a feeling of acute nervousness
> **Gobby**—being a loud mouth and/or offensive
> **Balls-up**—a messed up situation
> **Bob's your uncle** – You have made it.
> **Absobloodylutely** – Yes Indeed!
> **Dishy**—Hot/Sexually Attractive
> **Miffed**—upset or offended
> **Bobby Dazzler**—What U.K. male police officers used to call U.K. female police officers

Initially the WPS attracted complaints about how they behaved towards prostitutes and harassing them, but not taking any action against their clients. When the new commissioner, Sir Nevil MacReady, took over from Sir Henry he preferred the National Council of Women's Special Police Patrols opposed to the WPS. His reasoning was that there was no association with militant suffragettes, these patrols would be used instead, and actually formed the nucleus of the women police force.

The head of the Patrols was a Mrs Stanley and she had no love of the WPS as she felt that their uniforms and use of the Metropolitan Police ranks misled the public. Under her instigation the WPS were forced to change their name to the Women's Auxiliary Service (WAS) and in 1921 red flashes were added to their uniform so as to distinguish them from the Metropolitan Women Police Patrols.

In 1920, the Baird committee failed to recommend that the WAS should play any part in policing London and although they had made valuable contributions to the Royal Irish Constabulary during the "Irish Troubles", they were forced to suspend their activities. In 1940, they became inactive and were never revived.

In November 1918, Sir Nevil MacReady appointed Mrs Stanley as superintendent of the Metropolitan Women Police Patrols. They appointed 25 women, already in the Special Patrols and although they were never sworn in or given special powers of arrest they were employed directly under the orders of Scotland Yard and their prime responsibility were to Police.

During the time period of 1923-1930 Women Police were fully attested and given limited powers of arrest. In 1930-1969 A4 Branch (Women Police) was established under a female superintendent.

In 1969, the Branch was dissolved in advance of the Equal Pay Act was soon to change how women were perceived in the force. It wasn't until 1973 that policewomen were totally integrated into the Police Force and given equal pay, equal responsibilities and powers.

Maureen in the 1970s

CHAPTER ONE
Change in Career

At the age of 17 my life was full of fun. Lots of parties, boyfriends and nights out with the girls. I was happy in my current position as a secretary, but had just been asked to go for an interview with a French airline based in Victoria, London.

I went for the interview during my lunch break and whilst on my way back to my office a police officer walked around the corner on patrol with a policewoman. As we passed, he looked at me closely and smiled. After passing I looked back and he was doing the same.

My first thought was "Had I done something wrong?" We both kept on walking then it dawned on me that perhaps he was just giving me a second look because he was a young man...and I was wearing a very short mini skirt!

It humanized him and made me realize there was more to a uniform than what you saw, the person who wears it is human, has feelings, and is no different from anyone else. This started me thinking about the possibility of me actually being able to follow the idea of a new career.

My mother tells me that I always used to say as a child that I wanted to be a police officer, but as the years passed, I took other routes. My parents had a very conventional attitude as to education. They felt that a woman would leave school at 15 years old, get a job, and get married, and start a family. The man was intended as the money earner; therefore, my parents decided it wasn't worth me staying on at school to progress towards university, but to attend a secretarial college and obtain a career in that profession as my mother had.

As it turned out, my brother stayed on in education and was more suited to a "practical mechanical" career, whereas I would have loved the opportunity to take the opportunity to extend my knowledge in a professional field. Later on, I discovered my love of the law and I would have aimed at becoming a barrister in the law Courts of London. However, they say things happened for a reason and that was not my destiny.

I took the job at the air terminal and became Head Ground Stewardess which was a complete change in the previous secretarial roles I had held. This gave me the opportunity to make decisions and responsibility to manage the terminal when the manager was off duty. It wasn't long before one of the local officers would call in on his beat for a cup of coffee and check we had no problems. He was a really nice man and after some time he asked me out on a date, and I became very fond of him.

At the same time, my mother's friend's husband was a serving police officer in our neighbourhood. He pulled me to the side and asked if I had ever considered taking the step to becoming an officer.

I told him as a child I had always said that was my dream, but as time went on it sort of got pushed aside, so that opened the door for him to spike my interest in taking the next step and apply to join the force

When my boyfriend found out my decision, he was very unhappy about it, believing that it would change me as a person. Unfortunately, this disagreement, together with other circumstances, drove us apart and we stopped dating. Having to attend training school was going to take every minute of my day and there wasn't the time to continue in a serious relationship and that was my only regret in my decision to apply.

I had believed that you had to have obtained a high degree of education and exams, but as it turned out if you didn't have a degree then you had to take a very simple examine and a medical. Having passed both of those, the next step was interviews with very official high-ranking officers, both male and female.

After many interviews the numbers dwindled and after each set there were less and less people sitting in the office. Eventually, those left were told to go home and the board would send out notifications to all applicants notifying them of their decision.

At that moment in time had no possible idea that I would be accepted into the force, but that in three weeks I would be attending Hendon Police College and from then my life would never by the same.

Shock to the System

When the letter arrived, I still couldn't believe that I was being offered a position. Why I had doubts I can't say, I filled the criteria, passed the medical, and had good interviews…but a police officer? Was my dream really coming true? There it was in black and white… CONGRATULATIONS! I was accepted into a career and within three weeks my life would be totally different.

Three weeks was no time at all. My mother went into panic mode, convinced I was signing a death warrant on myself; my father was proud that I had taken an opportunity I always wanted; my friends were all amazed but pleased, with the exception of a few male acquaintances who were less than pleased. Living in the East End of London you couldn't help but have friends that were walking a very close line to being law breakers, so it pretty much meant that I wouldn't be seeing them much in the future.

Of course, handing my notice in to my employers got some comments!

Like anything you are looking forward to it takes forever for the time to pass, then all of a sudden you are on the eve of the event.

I packed a suitcase with everything would need for a three month stay, said goodbye to my mother and brother, and my father drove me to the address

> Definition of civvy. 1 civvies also civies plural : civilian clothes as distinguished from a particular uniform (as of the military) 2 : civilian.

in London where we were told to report. It was a time in my life that was interesting, exciting, but scary at the same time. On arrival, there were mainly men in the hall, and everyone had to introduce themselves to each other. A couple of women arrived and soon the influx of new recruits had all arrived. I felt as though had joined the Army, everything was so unlike 'civy' (civilian/unmilitary) life where people you were employed by were courteous and polite…but this was another world.

The next three months consisted of law, procedures, and various self-defense lessons, but it also had a great emphasis on working together as a team and being able to rely on the officer either side of you.

Our name was called and we were all loaded into a police coach, the men tended to sit together and the women as there were so few of us bonded together quite quickly.

The first stop was to New Scotland Yard which seemed too awesome and aloof. We were all trundled in and escorted to a large theatre style meeting room where we received a lengthy talk about the forthcoming training and schedules that we would be involved in.

Having had the job briefly explained, we all had to raise our left hand, place our right hand on the Holy Bible, and swear our allegiance to the Crown. It was done. I was now officially an officer in training with the London Metropolitan Police, sworn to protect and to uphold the law both on and off duty. It was now getting serious…

Baker Street Section House

At last we were taken to Baker Street where our home for the next three months was based. The house was kept in strict order by a female sergeant and on arrival we were welcomed and advised of the very strict rules in place and also told about consequences should we decide to break them…. gulp. She was a force to be reckoned with, she came from Scotland and was a very large lady who demand respect…and she got it. No one in their right mind wanted to cross this lady.

We were introduced to our roommates and settled in. Our bags were deposited and we were shown where the canteen was, where the laundry was, and then back to the canteen for lunch.

The women in charge of the canteen was a large lady from the West Indies, who we soon learnt hated the Police! A strange bedfellow indeed. Together with the fact the she became more aggressive at certain times of the month, it almost felt like taking your life in your hands when ordering your meal. No one complained about service or the menu, or a large carving knife was waived about to make sure we kept quiet.

Certain times she would show a sense of humor and some of the girls dared to tease her (with great care and ready to run.) She would laugh one minute, then scream like a banshee waving that knife the next! I heard that sometime later she actually took it a step further and attacked an officer with that knife...no great surprise that she was arrested and charged.

Our training would be starting almost immediately, but with some basics of getting us kitted out with supplies first so the tailor could work his magic.

I can't remember exactly where the tailor was; but it was in the bowels of London, close to the city where lanes spun of each other, dark and dingy streets where you could imagine Jack the Ripper working his deathly skills and disappearing a fast as he had appeared. The Tailors had been established in London forever and was responsible for all the police uniforms, and several of the larger hospitals in the area.

Having been measured from top to toes, I was given several crisp shirts and sets of detachable collars that you almost had to use a hammer on to even attempt denting them! had never seen such stiff collars, which were impossible to achieve yourself, so we knew that was a trip to the laundry. They looked smart but they were a killer on the neck and many times rubbed the skin raw because of their stiffness.

Next stop…shoes, and that was the next shock. Out came these leather shoes in my size. Today, it is rare to find leather soles, but these were made as they had been for years, leather throughout with laces.

I knew the job involved walking, but I never really thought about the shoes I'd be wearing. Somehow I had a feeling these were made for comfort and a truer words were never spoken. They turned out to be the most supportive shoes, you could walk for eight hours solid without complaining about your feet, they also were made to allow you to bull the toe caps (spit and polish shoes) which is something we learnt how to do from the ex-military guys in our group. That gave us points with the sergeant!

So, we were measured to our jacket and skirt, no trousers in those days, bought our shoes, given our shirts, collars and tie. Next came our cape, which was a warm fabric made for the colder days, and our Mackintosh for the rainy days, which of course in England there can be many. The last items or clothing was a pair of leather gloves, for keeping our hands warm or to protect our skin when doing searches or touching unpleasant things and last but not least, a domed hat, which over hung our eyes and protected our skull from flying objects.

After having finished with our fashion designer (and I say that very loosely) we headed back to our digs for what was probably the first, and last, night that we could actually relax, have a chat, and try to get to know the other females currently in situ (the group).

Of course, the other female officers that started their training several months prior to us took great delight telling us the horror stories of what we were likely to experience and how much study would be needed, of course we felt they were just kidding us...little did we know!

Our house was situated in Baker Street, not very far from the address that was famous for housing Sherlock Holmes. It had some great restaurants and clubs in the area so it was perfect for enjoying our time off. I didn't realize that basically we would have very little of that. Our day consisted from Monday-Friday getting up by six a.m., wash and get dressed, eat breakfast, then load into the coach for the one-hour drive across London to the College.

We would finish at five p.m. and get back to Baker Street by about six p.m. where we would change into civvies, eat dinner, do our washing/ ironing, bull up our shoes and study the famous Black Book.

The Black Book was the nickname given by us referring to the large black law book where all our knowledge of the law came from. Every part of a law had to be learned word-perfect and two-thirds of this book we would have to learn by heart to be able to pass our daily exams. Most of the questions we were asked had to be answered in the form stating the act it pertained to and what exactly was stated in that act.

Several months later the training school opted for a system which gave you four answers that you chose from... much easier, but I still would end up studying till the early hours making sure I knew the various powers of arrest and from where the power came from. I was loving it, and the love of the law became a passion for me.

The weekends gave a brief break from study, but many stayed opposed to going home so they could catch up with other jobs they needed to do. However, by staying there meant that if you were leaving the house you needed a pass and the time of return had to be before 11 p.m. If you failed to return on time the door was locked and bolted, and you had to wake up the sergeant to explain the reason for your tardiness! OMG that was quite an experience. I was 10 minutes late once, just once, never again, that was a horrifying experience, not because she did anything physically, but mentally she put the pressure on and for the next week, she'd get you up early and settle hints how we dared disturb her sleep...Even to this day have to smile as it surely taught me not to be late!

CHAPTER TWO
Training School

The next morning think we were all so excited at the prospect of our first day as a police officer in training. We were probationers, and that lasted for 2 years at which time we would be judged for our performance and report written by our senior officer as to whether we were fully accepted into the force.

We were up and ready quickly, breakfast eaten and then on to the busses for the first day of our career. At this stage we were still in "*civvies* until our uniforms were ready which would take about 2 weeks.

The police coach was ready to take us through London out to Hendon Police College where all our training would take place. We were first given a tour of the buildings, an old grand building surrounded by living quarters for the men. They deemed it not acceptable to mix the men and women in the living quarters, I was curious why they didn't trust us? Maybe they knew something we didn't, either way it meant our working day had two hours added to it traveling in and out of London in rush hour.

The ratio was astounding, about 10 female officers and 500 male officers...what odds! There were some really '*dishy* guys amongst them, but in truth there was no time for socializing in any shape or form. As I later found out getting up at six a.m. and working and studying till midnight left very little time for anything else. I started to understand that if the program was going to be workable all temptations had to be removed.

Having been sexed and classed (this is precisely how it felt) we were introduced to our first month's tutor. This sergeant was and gentle man with a pleasant manner and homely figure. He never raised his voice at us and always had a joke to tell, little did I know that in the future he was to become my brother in law.

Looking back, I think nearly every "*WPC* had a crush on him, he was so charming. His wife attended all functions, and made sure that any recruits were aware he had a wife, and was very married and that messing with her man was not a good idea.

The first hour of our lesson was delightful, we were missed books and a timetable was discussed. It was so relaxing when all of a sudden, the door burst open...Satan had arrived. It was like a stampeding bull had entered with steam coming out of his nostrils. The sergeant had us all stand to attention whilst he walked up and down the aisles of the classroom. After looking at us all with his steely grey eyes, he went to the front of the room and boomed at us to sit. He introduced himself as the chief inspector in charge of training and one by one had us stand to introduce ourselves.

From the moment we met him we knew he would take no prisoners.

This man meant business and from the moment he spoke to us we knew exactly where we stood. We would speak when spoken to, and not before. We would answer yes or no sir and nothing else, and certainly no one spoke if he was speaking or the sparks flew. I have never ever met a person who commanded such respect so quickly. Fear was part of it, but he never indicated what would happen to us if we disobeyed, you knew just not to. The underlying punishment was unspoken, and no one ever tried find out!

I never forgot the man or his position, but for a good reason. His aim was to have us act and think as one without questioning the command, a bit of a military style but in the last month of training when we all became a team he changed overnight. Once we were becoming officers in every sense of the word, he allowed us to see the kind, sensitive side he had in abundance. He was a lovely man who taught me the importance of self-discipline and I later discovered he had died of cancer, too young, and sad also that many other new officers would not have the benefit of his unique training.

Having experienced our first lesson in discipline we were filed out to the Parade Ground where we were told that every morning we were to file into our classes ready for inspection. Without fail at eight a.m. we would stand there, rain or shine, cold or heat, in full uniform ready for the commandant to inspect.

Everything was inspected, our hair (which couldn't touch the collar), nails, shoes and of course uniform.

After Inspection, we would then be marched around the parade yard for 30 minutes, which produced giggles and some tripping up. After lining up, we would stretch our arms out to touch our fellow officers' shoulder to space ourselves, eyes straight ahead. Once in place, then the drill sergeant took over. He was a strong muscular man with a very loud voice which he frequently used. Fortunately for us he had a sense of humor and often saw the funny side of events on drill sessions when he had '*newbie* probationers to train.

We would be marched until we got in step, unless *"Taffy"* wasn't in front. He was a gentle Welshman (hence the nickname) who stood about 6'7" with a very strong welsh accent and an inability to march with any rhythm. His arms would go in the same direction as his legs, opposed to swinging them left leg with right arm, and so forth. It was chaos because the one in the lead influenced those behind. Within minutes no one could march and being a smart mouth I called out for him to get it together.

Not the best thing could have done. The sergeant heard me and I was immediately brought to the front and told that if I could do any better then perhaps should take the parade.

You know I think that most children when they are at school believe that they spend several years of study has I hadn't realised the meaning of the word up until now One of the first pieces of equipment that we were given in the early days was a big black book. We all thought that it was a reference book, that it was, but not just for Reference, it was for learning, word-perfect. Most of it contained laws and procedures that we would he dealing with during our career, and in later years I realized the importance of such studying. We would have lessons during the day using the book and then homework set for the evening. Several acts and procedures would be set to learn word perfect and the following day we would be tested on it and required to be able to recite the homework word for wood from The Black Book.

On the first few evenings I couldn't believe that it would have been possible to learn so much in such a small amount of time. Once having travelled back to the Baker Street quarters, the time was taken up with all the jobs we had to do.

Normally we would get changed into casual clothes and head for the canteen and order our meal. Having battled with our anti-police Jamaican caterer, we would then iron our uniform, wash our shirts, and bull up our shoes till the shine reflected our faces.

That took a couple of hours, then everyone disappeared into one of the many comers to find their own space where they could concentrate on their study. Normally we would work solidly till about one a.m., reciting to ourselves the lines we knew we had to remember the next day. All the thoughts of dancing and partying till the early hours were long since forgotten, it was a lifetime away.

The next morning the same routine would unfold, and each morning it got harder and harder as the amount of sleep we were getting was lesser and lesser as each night we would get increased homework. On the weekends we would sleep through most of it together with studying those subjects that we had been given extra time for. Every morning the dreaded test on law and situations, which would show who had in fact done their homework?

You couldn't afford to not get it right as the next night there was more and more and more. Its amazing how much one is capable of learning in such a small amount of time, and of course if we hadn't to do so mach town cleaning and polishing, then we would have been able to use that time for The Black Book. However, rules were rules and I suppose looking back on my time at the college now I can see the value of pushing recruits in all directions. It certainly gave you the ability to be self-disciplined.

Of course, it wasn't all paperwork and study, we had to have practical experience, but of course they couldn't put us on the street literally, so they had to re-enact the situation to give us the feeling it was actually happening. So, we would take it in turns to be the public victims or officers. We would pretend to come upon a street accident or an assault or an allegation of some kind as we turned the corner.

We never knew what would be waiting them so we would walk the pretend streets and then deal with whatever we came upon. Of course, someone would be watching, marking us on how we handled the situation and what we did. If it were an allegation of some kind, then we would write a report and say how we would follow through on the case. There were many situations that we had been taught about, but just to keep us on our feet they would put together something that we hadn't precisely dealt with, just to see how we would improvise and deal with the problem in front of us.

The person playing the victim or person from the public would be given a scenario and you could not change their minds or alter what they had to told they should do so in fact it probably meant it was harder than dealing with the seal situation as they were told not to be persuaded or convinced about doing something else.

Of course, there was a reason behind keeping the women in Baker Street and the men in Hendon. With the ratio of to 50, respectively, I think they thought that a distraction of that magnitude in bedrooms next to each other would be too much, but of course they left nothing to chance. The rumour spread that the men we being fed "Bromide" in the form of an additive in the tea. True? Well I can't say, but I am sure the wives of some of the officers might have been suspicious when they came home at the weekend having been away for five days and not being interested in anything but sleep! Not that there was much time for doing anything that wasn't lying between pages!

It is surprising how quickly time passes when you are busy, and in no time, Christmas was slowly creeping up on us, not only signifying the end of our training, but the beginning of our two year probation period. Of course, Christmas was when we all could let our hair down and party, and party we did. It was decided a show was to be put on for all the officers and various people were cagouled into helping out.

For my part, I was persuaded to put a musical piece together using all the policewomen. That took some thought but eventually I decided that shock had its virtue and as we had spent that last 3 months being shocked in all directions, now it was our turn to turn the tables a little. Trouble was, it had to be done fairly tastefully as all the wives were coming and we had to be a little careful in what we presented.

So, I put on my thinking cap and came up with the idea of a nouveau way of performing "Top Hat, White Tie and Tails". All of the girls had their jackets on and no skirt, exposing legs all attired in fishnet stockings and suspenders. They had the male officers' helmets on and each had a truncheon that they would swing from their side.

It's surprising how a truncheon when used the "right way" can be a rather alluring tool! Well despite some misgivings on the dancing ability and rhythm of some of the WPC's we managed to pull it off. We were a great success and completed the first stage of my career which was to last a full seven years.

The beginning of real policing was about to start and I left the College with food memories, oodles of knowledge, and the naivety in the belief that we would make such a difference. As you will see in the following chapters had my work cut out for me...

Although we had survived the initial training, the next two years would be our probation period based on division under the wings of a fully qualified officer. We were now known as phase A Probationers and that we would remain until we took our final exams.

CHAPTER THREE
Police Areas

The Metropolitan Police covers the London areas, which starts in the central London area out towards the suburbs. Within the central London area there is a smaller force called the City of London Police Force, who basically have the responsibility to Police just the City, comprising mainly of the banking districts.

There is also the British Transport Police who have charge of policing all form of transport.

London being such a vast area was split into divisions to make the areas workable. A Division was in the center, which comprised Scotland Yard and many of the Embassy's and historic buildings including high Courts and Government offices. The policing in this Division was totally different from a Suburban Division as the further out you went, the area contained more residential and small businesses.

Each Division would have its own structure of rank, starting with constables, sergeants, inspectors, chief inspectors, superintendent, and chief superintendent. Each division chief would be responsible to higher ranking officers based in Scotland Yard. The ultimate being the Commissioner of Police.

Initially the Women's Police Department, prior to amalgamation and being totally integrated into the force, had their own chain of Female Senior officers that they were responsible to.

The woman police sergeant (also abbreviated as WPS) would ensure that all her female officers were put on various shifts to ensure that there was always at least one female officer available per division, especially on night duty.

Because there were so few policewomen on night duty you would cover two other divisions as well as your own so you were guaranteed to be busy. Once you had dealt with any situations, and a female was required to stay in the station cells overnight then they would employ a female matron to come to the holding station to attend to the prisoner until the court appearance. Not every station was equipped with cells so all female prisoners would be escorted to the station where they were equipped to secure the prisoners and have a matron on duty.

Where the Metropolitan area ended then the county force would have jurisdiction. Hampshire Constabulary has certain parts of their county covered by the

Metropolitan Force so it was a grey area at the borders. Most forces would work with each other to ensure that criminals crossing the borders would still be passed over to that force and then return them to the force where the offence took place.

Within each division there would be:

1. Beat officers on foot patrol covering set areas
   Responsibilities:

   Walking neighbourhoods and getting info on what was happening

   Dealing with possible local issues, school problems, shoplifters

   Giving tickets for double parking and double line infractions and of course the most favourite one of giving out tickets for no tax disc displayed or tax disc expired.

   At times those from above would target us to bring in a required number of tickets for the shift, so even when we would have preferred to have given a warning we had to choose the ticket option

2. Panda cars which had 1 or 2 officers driving a certain area

   Responsibilities:

   These officers would be sent out initially to all calls coming into the station and would determine if the could handle the situation or if it had to be passed to (C.I.D) – Criminal Investigation Department

3. Section sergeant car Responsibilities:

The sergeant on duty who would drive the areas ensuring all was in order; he was also available to attend situations where a decision was needed by a senior officer.

4. Area cars which covered the whole Division with two officers Responsibilities:

These received 999 emergency calls and if they needed support other mobile units in the area would be called to assist.

5. Traffic Division Responsibilities:

These cars were fitted with special equipment to enable them to measure speeds precisely and were primarily patrolled the street and motorways for speeding offences. They were also sent to the scenes of multiple accidents and serious crashes.

6. Criminal Investigation Division Responsibilities:

All Stations had an office for the C.I.D. officers. These are all plain clothed officers who deal with serious crimes where possible investigations and lengthy period of times are needed to find the criminal. All of these officers have served at least 2 years as a street cop and passed a board for approval to join that dept. They have their own rank of senior officers and work totally separate from the uniformed branch, however on many occasions they work with the uniformed officers as they often have information that can aid their investigations.

CHAPTER FOUR
On Division

In the last week of training school, we awaited eagerly the envelope that told us where we would be stationed and where we would live. So Christmas was spent with family knowing that after the new year we would be going to a new home and new work surroundings.

For those of you who have experienced having children, if you can remember the first day that you go home with your new baby and you are on your own, with help from the midwife and family but you have the responsibility of a mother and it is totally down to you as to your decisions with your child. That is how I felt, I was going out onto Division, with knowledge and the help of senior officers and a Sergeant but still, when on the street, people see a uniform and are totally unaware of how new you are to the job

My first post was Hendon, North London and I was housed in Bayswater, which was quite a journey every morning. Two buses through a very busy West Indian and Irish community. Wearing a Uniform was not advised so we travelled in civvies and changed on arrival.

My roommate was Maureen (another one) who I have remained friends with to this day. We were in a set of three very large Victoria Houses all joined together in Pembroke Square, set close to the Portobello Road Market and several good pubs. We shared a room for several months until a single room became available which gave us both a little more privacy, especially if we were on opposite shifts.

The house was supposed to be haunted and to this day I remember several things of a ghostly nature that happened there that could not he explained. It again had a Wander an elderly policewoman doe for retirement who made sure that the house rules were followed. No boyfriends could be seen to kiss you on the doorstep, you had to bring them in to the sitting room. So, on a Saturday night Warden and boys were waiting to go into the room just to kiss goodnight. Any visitors had to sign in and no overnighters allowed. Well not officially and on more than one occasion males were seen to be creeping out, tiptoeing past the Warden's door. To be caught out was more than your life was worth. In those days it was deemed to be "letting the honour of the force down, oh how things changed over the next few years.

The house or should I say houses were joined by two corridors and there were officers living there from all over London. At that time there were very few mixed living quarter. There were the new officers aged nineteen years old and up and then them were some officers in their fifties and nearing the end of their career.

I have to say, at this point that m very open minded as to people's sexual preferences, but prior to our arrival there had been a big clearout of officers. Nobody wanted to speak of it but apparently at one stage in the early 60's the female commander was and the had inclined to recruiting women that had the same sexual tendencies. It resulted in a lot of well-built very masculine females being recruited, as being feminine was not a quality she recognised as necessity or a requirement to be in the force.

She had long since retired when the current commander, who was married to a Vicar served complaints from a local gay club in Bayswater that it had been raided by the police. He pointed out that a lot of his clientele lived in the section house in question. There was uproar and the brass was flying around in droves. A meeting was held at the section house and it was made clear that what people did in their own time was their own business. However, any behaviour that would throw the force into a bad light would not be tolerated. No behaviour of this nature would be tolerated while living in the Section House and that if officers wanted to stay in their jobs then it was suggested that they might like to move to private residences to avoid bringing the force into disrepute.

Overnight the accommodation emptied out, leaving numerous rooms vacant. No more was said and everything was brushed under the carpet. That was another change for the better, in the 60's sexual preferences was deemed a source of shame if it didn't fit in. Whereas now, there are clubs within the force for supporting the gay offices and offering support for any that feel that they are being persecuted because of it. That is how it should be, but I lived through a totally different experience

We were still not deemed equal and the quality act had yet to be passed. One of the first lessons you had to learn was that women were deemed as a necessity for dealing with women and children, besides that, they were tolerated. We were also often teased and ridiculed and if you couldn't take the heat then get out of the kitchen. This attitude was often verbalized by our male colleagues, especially those at the end of their career. They saw us as baby makers and husband getters, why else would we want to do this job? Why indeed, many times I had to have my wits about me with a quick answer, and not show any shock or disgust. The moment you did, it would worsen until they could reduce the WPC to tears.

Once you retaliated and gave as good as you got, then they respected you and left you alone. Part of me understands that mentality, if you can't take abuse from your fellow officers then you certainly would not be able to take it from the community and they meant what they said. Of course, you shouldn't have to take abuse from anyone, and I don't condone that, but that is how it was and WPC's in the 60's and 70's took it as part of their job and there was nowhere to take it anyway. In today's force, there are sexual harassment claims and all sorts of other acts that protect females in the workplace. Back then, it didn't exist. The only good thing about it was is it made you stronger. What is it they say "What doesn't kill you makes you stronger? Well that certainly was the case then.

My friend was based in Harlesden, another North London station and during the night duties we both covered each other's are due to the shortage of female officers

At that time policewomen, often got slotted into the typical "female" jobs such as shoplifters, children, and young person. So, they always had to have a police officer covering, or at least available at a station should the need arrive.

The first day at my station it was quite obvious that I was being scrutinised by the various shifts. Most of the senior officers, including my duty sergeant had the belief that the only reason a woman joined the job were to find a man...how wrong could you be. Most boyfriends prior to joining and ones that met only had to hear what your job was and they were off like a scalded rabbit. Unless they were police officers they had no comprehension about what we were about

Of course, not only did have to prove myself to the numerous male officers I had to undergo the C.I.D. approval. In those days there was quite a gap between the two departments, and a lot of resentment. Being a woman made it even worse so it was inevitable that not long after I arrived I was put to the test.

In those days I smoked a little (e.g. when under stress) and this occasion it was becoming a little stressful. Our office was only two doors up from the C.I.D. office and I mislaid my matches. I now think they were takes so that I had to go look for some others. I called in their office to ask to borrow the matches, which they were so keen to give me and I took them back to the office. Whether they realised it or not, I had a terrible fear at that stage of spiders so it was of great delight to them that their little they had put up for me worked a treat. Inside the matchbox they had managed to squash in the most enormous spider that I have seen, so big that as I opened the box it sprung out so quickly that was left screaming and running from the room. The only thing that stopped me running down to the front office was the roar of laugher that could hear coming from the next office.

They were more than happy to have proved that I was a "mere" silly girl, and that scream cost me a lot more effort to prove that I could do the job.

Still they had their fun and looking back now must admit it was quite funny, it just didn't feel like it at the time.

As a new constable, the first two years you were attached to another officer who had experience of more than two years so you were known as a phase A Probationer. During this time I underwent constant training, tests, and reviews. It probably was the most interesting time, career wise, as I was able to expand my knowledge whilst at the same time putting that into practice. I soon qualified as a First Aider with St. Johns Ambulance and then as an official fingerprint officer. I attended a driving school where we were schooled in the art of driving under hazardous conditions, such as chases and observations, and had to qualify again in this new medium.

In the late 60's Policewomen were responsible in the station for any children, babies, or women that were brought into the station, and therefore, received extra training in dealing with children & young persons. There was a special Act in Law that protected this part of society, which need specialized knowledge, and as a woman police officer, it was part of my training to learn this side of the job.

Most male officers that brought anyone included in this group into the station would call for a woman police officer and pass the case over to us. So, it was quite early in my career that I came into contact with the many sad cases of child neglect and abuse that seems to be a growing disease of modern society.

Its strange bow the body reacts when it doesn't get enough sleep, but also how hard it is to get used to doing three weeks of nights straight off.

Shifts were three weeks nights and then six weeks of late and early shifts. My eating times get totally out of sequence and I never got used to eating my main dinner at six a.m.! Of course, night times were when the worst neglect cases came to light and the time when most of social services are in bed, leaving us having to handle things on our own until other social departments awoke and helped with placements.

During night shifts, policewomen at my station covered three to four divisions across the northern part of London, S. Q and Y division (as it was then) were mainly the ones covered, so our nights were normally spent hopping from station to station. Different areas had different types of problems, some of them had large concentrations of different cultures such as Indian, West Indians, and Irish, to name a few. Each culture had to be handled differently as their perceptions of what was allowed and not allowed did not necessarily fit in well with English Law. It was a great experience handling all the difference types of problems that arose but also sometimes very sad ones.

The Kilburn area housed a high population of Irish that had come over to England to work on the many building sites. Many were single young men who having been paid on a Friday night, would then all congregate in the many Irish pubs in Kilburn to spend their hard earned money.

I have to smile at the events that often happened on a Friday night regularly. At about closing time it was a normal occurrence for the police to get a call to the High Street deal with fighting youths. No weapons just overzealous males, drunk and punching everything around them. Quite often the van would take a couple of WPC's with them in case any women were present and when it was seen that it was fairly straightforward, the men sometimes would keep a distance and get the women to go up to them and ask them quite calmly to come with them to the station. (in other words, we were arresting them). It was done in such a way that quite often they would call over all to those that were fighting and invite them to fall into the van, without a blow being levied anywhere, then the men took over. If the policemen had gone in first, they would have had a worse fight on their hands.

The next morning, often the men when being released would pass us and apologise for anything untoward they had said, or any swear words they might have used. I doubt if the same courteous behaviour would be repeated today.

It was at this station that my first dealing of neglect came to light.

I was called over to a station where a young seven-year-old was found drunk in the gutter. They found out his address whilst he was in hospital having his stomach pumped. I went to the address with another male officer.

The house was in total darkness and the front door ajar. Armed with only touches we called out but no one answered. All we heard was the faint whimpering of a child somewhere in the house.

It was quite apparent from the smell that hit us as we entered the property that we were going to find some pretty unpleasant condition. The officer was with was a quite new and had little experience was with neglect in his time in the force. The entrance floor had gaps that we had step over and there was seemingly no working electricity. To together just the moonlight and our torchlight we progressed into the first room.

If I could bottle the smell that hit us, of years of dirt, urine and excreta, then it might just explain the condition of the house. In the lounge, one light bulb that worked and a small television in the corner of the room that was switched on.

In the room were several derelict chairs and settees, all of which were hanging together by bare threads and wires. On one of the chairs there were three young children huddled together, next to them was a plate of moldy stale bread. In that meagre light their tattered, unclean and underfed condition was the sorriest sight I have ever seen and will stay with me forever. We reassured them and asked where their parents were, "out," was all they replied. We ventured into the "kitchen" and to this day I can describe and remember vividly what hit me.

There were several cupboards, a sink, a fridge and a cocker. In the corner there was a pile of clothes, or should I say rags, shoulder high. On the work surfaces there were piles of stale rotten food and dirty dishes in the sink. The cooker had layers of fat and grease burnt into it and appeared to have something move across the surface. As I shone my torch on the surface I saw the hundreds of maggots that had made this their home. The fridge had nothing but rotten food in it and a pile of salt head.

I continued through to the next room, and to what was supposed to be a W.C. The flush had stopped working a long time ago and everything was overflowing on to the floor. At this stage, I was glad I hadn't eaten. I immediately put a call into the station to tell them what I had found and to call an ambulance to take the children to hospital as they were so weak and sickly I didn't want to chance taking them to the station before they had been checked over by the duty doctor.

I left my colleague with the three children downstairs and started up the stairs. Many of the stairs were missing and it took a great deal of care to avoid the broken pieces of wood. As I got closer to the top of the stairs, the whimpering I heard earlier started again. I went from room to zoom with only one light working on the whole of the top floor. In the shadow of one room I could see a cot in the moonlight and sitting in the corner was the tiniest little might. She was covered in sores and sitting in urine sodden sheets. I dreaded to think what or when the child was last fed. With the best blanket I could find, gently lifted the child into my arms where she clung on, scared and hungry.

At that precise moment, I could not any forgiveness for the parents that could put their children through such trauma. There could be no excuse acceptable in a society where help is given when asked for.

I checked quickly the other rooms and ascertained there were no more children and headed carefully down the stairs. By this time the ambulance had arrived and looked over the four children. Two of them were in need of hospitalisation and two were fit enough for us to take them back to the station where we could look after them until someone from Social Services could find them a place of safety.

Numerous officers were arriving, some to take pictures of the house and its condition, and others to question the neighbours as to the whereabouts of the parents.

On returning to the station, it was decided that an officer should remain at the house should the parents return. It was then my job to look after the two little ones and contact social services to arrange a place for them to stay until we could ascertain what would happen long term.

At about two a.m. the children were taken to a safe house and shortly afterwards the parents came scurrying into the station. The father had been out with his new girlfriend and the mother had been down at a pub drinking, leaving the seven-year-old to watch the others, all of which were younger than him. Both parents were angry and abusive to officers, accusing them of interfering in things that didn't concern them.

The fact their seven-year-old was drunk and in need of a stomach pump and their four other babies were living in total squalor, and totally unsupervised seemed to go right over their head.

Of course, the following weeks were spent obtaining medical reports from doctors and hospitals listing the number of diseases and skin complaints the children had, all brought on by the conditions they were forced to live in. It came to light that a child service group were indeed visiting the family over the previous months. The young university graduate felt that the mother was trying and lack of funds was responsible for their living conditions. I expect many families that had small incomes and large families would take great offence as I did to this reasoning. Cold water cost nothing, and that would at least keep things clean.

If the parents could afford to smoke and spend nights out at the pub, then they could afford food for their children.

What I had witnessed was like a scene out of *Oliver Twist* and the worst of workhouses where neglect was common practice and no social help available.

Of course, the week passed for the case to be put before the judges and eventually the case was ready.

So much time and effort was made to try and do the best for those children. During which time the parents did nothing but scream and abuse any officers from any department that tried to sort out their problems.

Eventually, after many hours of describing and presenting reports, the parents were fined and put on probation.

The result of which they were given a new council house, the children were returned to them, and they were told to look after their children properly.

Everyone was flabbergasted at the inadequacy of this decision. Why would a new house change the attitude of the parents? However, this was the first hard lesson I had to learn that no matter how much you do towards trying to help someone, as an officer you have to abide by the court's decision and trust that things will improve.

However, I cannot help wonder how these children grew up, whether they survived and became responsible adults, or whether what they knew was what they felt to be the norm and would in the future behave and live in the same way as they had been forced to be brought up.

So many times, I have wondered why a person should want to bring a child into the world and abuse them so badly. I still do not have the answer.

Another part of training, which I must say was not compulsory, was a visit to the local mortuary where you could see how procedures were carried out. It was decided between several of the female officers that they would like to know how they would react on seeing a dead body, best to know if you were going to pass out or not. Not the ideal thing for an officer if you came across one on your travels.

It was planned and off we went to the local offices run by the council. It was a very clinical cold set of rooms (for obvious reasons). In one room there were several marble slabs and all sorts of equipment which I didn't want to see again in my lifetime, yet had a pretty good idea if I died an unnatural death, would indeed see me.

In the other room were numerous stainless-steel cupboards, which without any notice, the guide opened up for us. Inside there were several drawers, like an enormous freezer and in each drawer there was a pair of feet, all with a nametag attached to the big toe. At this sight, one of the girls nearly fainted, a male officer ran out to vomit and several of us went a lighter shade of pale.

I remember this moment in time as if I had taken a picture and kept it in my wallet. I can shut my eyes and see that room, those feet and the first young dead body of my career.

I managed to breathe deeply and steady myself. "Come on now girl, this is your job, detach yourself whilst doing it," and that is how I managed every time. Our tutor wheeled out a tray where a young man no older that 20 years old was lying. A perfect form, agile looking, and handsome with dark curly hair.

He looked so peaceful; it was uncanny that this had been a living breathing person not long ago. This man in fact was a university student who couldn't face selling his parents that he wasn't going to pass his final exams, and rather than face failure he chose death. How sad. If nothing else that taught me one thing, whatever children I had, no matter what they did in life, I never wanted them to be afraid of telling me anything, regardless of what might think or say. Hopefully mine grew up knowing that.

The next couple of paragraphs might be a little distasteful or disturbing to some so void them if you feel that it might upset you. The details are graphic.

The autopsy was another thing that is best not dwelt on. As an officer of the law if you were the officer finding the body then by law you had to present at the autopsy to ensure continuity of evidence. After the first few then it actually became interesting although gruesome at times. The removal of the face sounded as though it would be a difficult thing to do and yet once having removed the top of the skull, the train would be placed in a receptacle and weighed. Then the purity would be removed. The skin covering the face was then pulled down leaving tissue and muscle with no sign recognizable of the person that was lying there.

The smell of burning bone as the saw was used, is a smell not pleasant, but the sound of the tongue being ripped out was absolutely repulsive. It was at this point my stomach started to turn cartwheels. Obviously, all organs would be removed and weighed after opening up the rib cage. All notes were made during this procedure and cause of death was ascertained. In a regular, unsuspicious death then this would be the norm. The procedure in cases of suspicious death or murder was handled differently as more care would be needed for evidence. Once the autopsy was done then the organs, including the brain, would be put back into the stomach cavity and everything else was stitched into place, including the face and skull.

When I looked at the person afterwards I would have never known what had proceeded, and thankfully the family members would be unaware. However, I have to say hate the thought of being a subject on a slab, but I am hoping that won't be looking down from above watching it

The only time that was unbearable was when you had to present at a child's autopsy, one who had been the subject of violent death. I never did get used to that nor could I find it interesting

Many hours of policing were spent on the beat. Walking a set route, giving a presence of law in the community. Of course, we were expected as well to look out for traffic violations such as packing on yellow lines, unauthorized parking, and the inevitable failing to display a current tax disc. That was my most hated role and it did nothing to improve public relations. For my part, I would rather have cautioned offenders, given them an official warning with a time period to get their tax, and of course to immediately move their vehicle. Unfortunately, the duty sergeant did not agree and every time you came back you would have to port how many tickets you had issued. If you didn't hit the required amount you were sent back out to get more and you didn't dare to come back without some.

This would happen rain or shine, cold or hot, there were very few "panda" cars, a name given in the mobile patrols attached to the station. The area car would patrol but was used for emergency call and not general police duties. Today, you very rarely see a foot patrol officer due to lack of numbers and the amount of work needed to be done quickly in large spread areas so nearly every officer is mobile. I think that that is a shame because rural areas found a security in knowing their local beat officer. You would get invited into shops for a cup of tea or a sandwich if lunch time. Lots of information was forwarded to us and it helped us know exactly what was going on in the community.

That is now lost and I don't think that it is a good thing. Now officers are strangers, the confidence isn't there and people don't open up as much. I suppose it is a sign of the times.

CHAPTER FIVE
Black Museum

The Crime Museum Origin

The Prisoners Property Act of 1869 gave authority for police to retain certain items of prisoners' property for instructional purposes, but it was the opening of the Central Prisoners Property Store on 25th April 1874 that provided the opportunity to start a collection. The store was housed in No. 1 Great Scotland Yard, which was at the rear of the commissioner's office at No. 4, Whitehall Place.

The idea of a crime museum was conceived by an Inspector Neame who had already collected together a number of items, with the intention of giving police officers practical instruction on how to detect and prevent burglary. It is certain that by the latter part of 1874, although it was not described as such, a museum of sorts was in existence. It was later that year that the official authority was given for a proper crime museum to be opened.

Inspector Neame, with the help of a P.C. Randall, gathered together sufficient material of both old and new cases to enable a proper museum to be opened. The actual date when it opened in 1875 is unknown, but the permanent appointment of Neame and Randall to duty in the Prisoners Property Store on the 12th April suggests that the museum came into being in the latter part of that year.

There was no official opening of the museum, and two years elapsed before we found a record of the first visitors. This was on the 6th October 1877 when the Commissioner Sir Edmund Henderson, KCB, accompanied by the assistant commissioners, Lt. Col. Labolmondiere and Capt. Harris, visited with other dignitaries. By now, there was a steady increase in the number viewing the displays and the first visitors book, which spans some eighteen years from 1877 to 1894, reads like a current Who's Who'. Certainly not all visitors were asked to sign the visitor's book, but as instruction in the museum was part of CID training, the museum was in constant use.

In 1877, the name Black Museum was coined, when on the 8th April a reporter from *The Observer* newspaper used the term after being refused a visit by Inspector Neame. However, the museum is now referred to as the Crime Museum.

In 1890, the museum moved with the Metropolitan Police Office to new premises at the other end of Whitehall, on the newly constructed Thames Embankment. The building, constructed by Norman Shaw RA, and made of granite quarried by convicts on Dartmoor, was called New Scotland Yard. A set of rooms in the basement housed the museum and, although there was no Curator as such, PC Randall was responsible for keeping the place tidy, adding to exhibits, vetting applications for visits and arranging dates for them. The museum was closed during both World Wars, and in 1967, with the move of the Metropolitan Police Headquarters to new premises in Victoria Street, S.W.1, the museum was housed in rooms on the second floor. In 1981, a new redesigned museum was opened on the first floor.

The Present Museum

The present museum is in two rooms. The first contains an extensive collection of weapons, all of which have been used in murders or serious assaults in London, and displays items from famous cases, generally prior to 1900, such as Jack the Ripper and Charlie Peace. A morbid display, which attracts comment, is the display of the death masks of people hanged at Newgate Prison, which adorn a high shelf and look down on visitors. The second room contains cabinets under the following categories:

0. Famous Murders
0. Notorious Poisoners
0. Murder of Police Officers

- Royalty
- Bank Robberies
- Espionage
- Sieges
- Hostages and hijacking

Famous cases shown in the museum include:

- Ruth Ellis
- John Reginald Halliday Christie
- The Stratton Brothers
- John George Haigh
- **Neville Heath**
- Dennis Nilsen
- Dr. Neil Cream
- Dennis Nilsen
- Mr. & Mrs. Seddon
- **Dr. Crippen**
- Craig
- Bentley

The museum is not open to members of the public, but is now used as a lecture theatre for the curator to lecture police and like bodies in subjects such as Forensic Science, Pathology, Law and Investigative Techniques.

Many dignitaries have visited the museum include Gilbert & Sullivan, Sir Arthur Conan Doyle, Harry Houdini, The Prince of Wales (later to be Edward VII), Stan Laurel and Oliver Hardy, Jerome K. Jerome, EW. Hornung and members of the Royal Family.

So this was now considered an important part of our

education and our trip to the museum was secured.

The curator at the museum was an officer who had done his early years of service on Division and now had the privilege of this prestigious posting. No shifts, no bank holidays, and staying in the dry. A pretty good job for someone who was nearing retirement. He was of the old school of officers who made it quite clear that women were not suited to this "man's force" and as soon as we started the tour he indicated that there was a locked door at the rear of the museum where the worst crimes and evidence were kept in an extra secure location to ensure that those of a 'sensitive nature' might not want to see.

With that he looked directly at the only two females in the room indicating that it might be better if we did not go into this room. That was like a red flag to a bull and there was no way they were going to keep us out when all our classmates were going in and he didn't.

I was always fascinated by museums, but this held even more interest for me now and the next couple of hours saw things that will never forget. All the famous criminals and murderers that had only ready about over the past years were now in front of my very own eyes, details of the crimes that only officers dealing with the case would have had access to Evidence consisting of photos, weapons and the tools that were used to commit those crimes.

Pictures of the bodies of the victims that were explicit in the most intimate ways and the evidence used to convict those criminals. I was totally mesmerized by what saw and to this day can close my eyes and see that room and evidence.

I suppose that might mean that had a form of a traumatizing effect for those memories to last for so long.

Of course, police officers are renowned for their sense of humour that can be a little extreme, and this trip only encouraged them to step it up, and they did, making comments at various times during the viewing. Of course, the curator had heard it all before and he just rolled his eyes every time one of the men made what they considered was original joke over one of the items.

The burglary section was particularly interesting. I had gone into this section believing that a lot of burglaries occurred because the owner of the property had been a little relaxed in security and had either put on poor locks, or just forgotten to secure the premises. Here were the tools of the trade and were they surprising. These tools showed that there was no lock unlockable, and even lock put in unusual places, there was a way to get to them. The minds of those inventing these tools had to be admired. How on earth they came up with the ideas I had no idea. Some went through a simple letterbox, turned different angles, expanded upwards, pinchers would emerge and then the lock latched onto and pulled back. So many locks, and so many opposite numbers that can unlock them.

After seeing this section, I was totally convinced that anybody's home could be broken into. This definitely made me feel insecure and owning a large Rottweiller was the bet source of defense together with a very loud alarm system.

Jack the Ripper's section was totally mesmerizing, the evidence and the pictures showing how horrific his crimes were and how because the period in time had no access to today's modern technology, Ripper was never caught and brought to justice. Recently, a book written by Patricia Cornwell, who took time out of her normal style of forensic science books to investigate evidence collected, used modern technology to try and trace who in fact the Ripper was. In my mind I believe she found out who he was and when you read the book yourself then you will see all the reasoning behind her findings.

We were given a second chance to decline going into the locked room, but by now there was nothing on earth could have prevented the women officers from going in. This now was a challenge by our male counterparts, which during my whole time in the service would have to get used to.

The cabinets, locked and secured, protecting important and ancient history that if lost or stolen could never be replaced. Shocking it was, but I was also fascinated when it got to the sexual perversion section. There were numerous outfits made of leather and black patent leather that had sharp studs embedding into them so that when the person wore the item they would cut into the skin, the more pressure applied the greater the damage.

Pain and sex, now the sex could understand but to

link it with so much pain and bodily harm could not, yet here it was, the evidence of a dark side of human nature. The whips laden with nails, bondages that would be used in the darkest of sex acts. In one section there was a record player, totally out of place to be in this part of the museum, next to it had a long arm that was attached to the end of the needle arm. Next to the player was an arrangement of plastic penises varying in size. This had to have an explanation and one that we wanted to hear.

Apparently, a young couple had devised a device that whilst playing music on the record player had an attachment on the needle arm that moved back and forth together with the needle movement. The faster music played, the faster the arm thrust in and out. You can see where I am going with this, I am sure, as we certainly did when was explained to us. They had a members club with a high charge for attending the performance. The wife would be strapped to a table and the player placed between her thighs. The player would be capable of three speeds, slow, medium, and fast. Members would choose the music and the size of the penis that was attached to the arm. Then the performance would begin, and the woman would writhe and have multiply orgasms to the applause of the audience.

I have to say that the largest of the penises was quite impressive by any standard and this was the one favoured by the members. I would have thought that the size of this must have been painful but of course from the performance standards added a little more interest. This had gone on for several months and they had earned a large sum of money. This might have continued without anyone knowing what went on behind the locked doors of a suburban house, had it not been for a small incident.

They decided to up the performance and wanted to make it more interesting, so to perfect it they needed to practice. On this occasion the husband tied her up in a slightly more provocative position and placed the machine ready for the practice session. This time he was using the largest of the models and started the machine up. What happened then was a chain of events that couldn't have been foreseen. He got an urgent call to go visit his mother who had been taken to the hospital with a suspected stroke and in his panic rushed out forgetting that his wife was tied up with the machine in full swing. The wife started to get uncomfortable, and not realizing her husband had left the house tried to move her legs, inadvertently she knocked the speed lever on to the fastest setting and at that point her pain and discomfort increased. She was basically having sex with a machine that was not going to stop. After a short while of this she began crying out for her husband to stop the machine as she was in pain. Of course, her cries went unheard and the machine was still turning at 78r.p.m. It wasn't long before she was beginning to experience sharp stabbing pains in her vagina and the skin surrounding the area was beginning to tear and bleed.

She was slipping in and out of consciousness and the damage to her was increasing. With the remainder of her breath before passing out she gave out one more scream, which fortunately was heard by neighbour who then phoned the police. When the officers arrived, they broke in to find this strange set up.

Of course, she was taken to hospital and the equipment used was confiscated and taken away for evidence. Charges were brought against both of the couples and I am sure that many a crude joke was passed around amongst those dealing with that case.

Pictures in this museum were extremely gruesome showing in great detail the horrific crimes that have been the subject of films and conjecture. Pictures of the remains of bodies that had been cut up and put in acid, bodies buried in the garden, and many other such crimes.

Once you got used to the shocking details that the evidence supplied, it was fascinating and I am sorry to say that this type of exposure made you a little more hardened to tragedy and murder. Was that a good thing? Probably not, but I had many such incidents to follow that this type of exposure helped me to deal with the circumstances that surrounded this type of case.

CHAPTER SIX
Ghostly Happenings

So now only one week to go out of the three-week night shift, and it had been very busy few weeks on nights and I had spent 12 hours every night hopping from station to station dealing with a variety of different situations.

This was nearing the end of the week and we experienced a full-blown power cut where everyone in the town lost electricity. We were sitting around the station with candles when a call came in alleging that some strange noises had been heard by some residents in an old Victorian house at the bottom of the town.

Not knowing whether this could involve male or female it was decided to send one of each of us. Anyway, I was bored and I could do with the walk.

Armed with torches, we started our very dark walk down the town with nothing but the moon to give us light. It was quite a walk, nothing but the light from a very full moon that disappeared every time a cloud passed over.

Eventually we found the house number we were looking for and climbed the steps to the front door. We rang the bell of the complainant and after hearing whom we were pushed the buzzer to let us in. When we went to his flat door and knocked, he opened the door very slightly, still unsure who we were. Seeing the uniform, he confirmed that it had indeed been him who had rung to complain about strange noises and added that they seemed to be coming from the top flat. He also added that he hadn't seen that particular tenant for a while so he thought it strange that he should hear any noises from there.

We had four long flights of stairs to climb, in total darkness albeit we had torches, they only gave a small amount of light and only in the area they were pointed at. The effect was quite eerie; they cast shadows up and down the stairs reflecting in the windows on the landings. By this stage my colleague decided to lead the way and I am not ashamed so say that I held on to the back of his jacket firmly instructing him not do anything stupid like trying to make me jump! My nerves at this stage were getting quite on edge, my fear of the darkness starting to rear its ugly head. I knew that selling my kid brother all those ghost stories at bedtime and scaring the hell out of him would return and get their revenge…

As we reached the top floor, we could see that the top flat's door was slightly ajar, and a trickle of light was sent through intermittently as the clouds passed over the moon. One moment we had half-light, the next total darkness and the suddenness of it made the eyes almost blind for a split second.

As we reached the door we tapped on it, calling out, hoping for the occupants to answer. No reply. This time we said we were the police and had come to check on strange noises. Silence. We both knew we had to go in and investigate; yet neither of us was keen to do so. We looked at each other, neither of us too sure of what to expect, but being a lady, I decided that it would be best if he went in first. Was he glad, I don't think so. By this time, we both had fired up our imaginations. When we eventually fully entered the room, we were greeted with a totally dark room.

As we shone our torches slowly around the room, the clouds cleared and the moon shone through directly on to the bed in front of us. In the bed there was outlined a human form, one that was not moving.

"Maybe he was a heavy sleeper," my colleague suggested. "Maybe not," I said. We both moved slowly towards the bed at which time the moon chose to disappear again leaving just our torches. We pointed the beam at the figure, and the ghostly face looking up at the ceiling with open dead eyes left us frozen to the spot. It was quite obvious this life had left some time earlier and we both very quickly decided to leave the room to phone the station.

The speed at which we retreated was no less than gazelle like, both trying to reach the door first. Just as we both reached the door a large gasp like sound came from behind us from the direction of the bed. We both froze. We looked at each other and slowly turned round. By this time every hair on my body was standing to attention, my throat was dry, too dry to scream and my heart felt as though it was sitting at the back of my throat pumping for all its worth.

What met our gaze sent us running from that room and down the four flights of steps three at a time. The figure was slowly sitting upright, groaning as he did so. His eyes stared straight ahead and the rays of the moon again outlined his white colourless face. After a short period, which to us seemed to be forever, he slowly laid back down exhaling air with a ghastly gagging sound.

Having both reached the pavement we stood their shaking for a moment, knowing fail well that we had witnessed this dead body expelling gases trapped inside; nevertheless, it was one of the scariest moments that I have ever experienced and should have appeared in a hammer movie. It was not what I had expected to encounter on a normal tour of duty.

Little did I know that this would be one of many such incidents that I, as an officer, could expect.

It seemed that this tour of night duty was going to give me a full-blown sample of what could expect. One week later exactly I was called to a house with another officer, again just like the horror movies which the Americans have great delight in having the heroines always walk into a dark flat, no lights. This time unsuspecting, I walked into the hallway of a house and before we could put any lights on, I was met by a pair of very cold feet tapping me on the side of my face.

As I slowly looked up I saw the sad figure of a man who had decided that the world was too much for him and he decided to end it all. A note by the side of him told us that he had in fact terminal Cancer and could not suffer the pain anymore. I could understand his actions but I am sure that he would not have wanted his parents so have suffered the pain and anguish they did when had to deliver the news to them.

One thing learnt early on in my career is that the force has a humour all of its own, sometimes a little sick, but I found out later that this was part of the shield officers put up to protect themselves for the tragedy that they dealt with. It took some getting used to but slowly you would start to understand the jokes and laugh at incidents that an outsider would think very strange.

One late afternoon a new constable attended a suicide with a number of other male officers. A young man had jumped in front of a train from a bridge. Of course, the body was spread over a large area and the officers' job was to retrieve as much as they could. After a time, most parts were found except for the head. The officers all left leaving the new officer to find the head with the instruction that the van would come back for him when he called

After some time, the officer spotted the head, which although was bruised was in fairly good, recognisable shape. Close by he found a fire bucket and placed the head on top of the sand in the bucket. He tried to call the officer, but his battery had gone flat. He walked up to the station entrance and waited for about 30 minutes and realized that the van was not going to come back he decided that he would take a bus back to the station not a good decision. He was pleased with his find and was eager to prove to his colleagues that he was a valued member of the team. Unfortunately, sitting on the bus with the bucket beside him with a pair of dead eyes looking up at every passenger passing him proved to be a really bad decision. The bus stopped and passengers jumped off the bus screaming and vomiting. The police were called and he got not only a lift back to the station but a very severe talk about bad judgement. I was slowly learning that male officers had acquired in this job a strange sense of humour and often initiation was something they enjoyed when a new officer joined the station. Fortunately, the next test did not involve me.

Whilst sitting having my much-earned cup of coffee, the station received a call from one of the officers on patrol. The station collapsed in a fit of laughter, everyone was beside themselves, so much so they couldn't explain what had just occurred. After they calmed down they explained or rather started to when a very white faced young officer staggered into the station looking highly shaken. Again, the station fell about laughing. It appeared that this new officer had mentioned to another that he was scared of the dark and believed in ghosts. Oh what an admittance.

So as one of the biggest cemeteries was in Holloway, the officers could not resist setting up a little treat for their latest addition.

Apparently, an officer had hidden in the graveyard, draped in chains and white sheets whilst the station pretended to get a call stating that some "strange happenings" were taking place at the cemetery. Two officers were despatched, one being this new officer. On arrival, the older officer suggested they split up and one go one way and the other go another. Reluctantly, the new officer unwittingly headed off in the direction of the ghostly apparition that was due to appear. In the dead of night, with a full moon, as he made his way between the headstones, this undercover officer started to groan and rattle his chains. Slowly he rose behind the headstone close to this officer, who on seeing this immediately emptied both bowels and bladder and ran screaming from the place.

British Slang Definitions

Cock-up—Screw up	**Minted**—to be wealthy
Rubbish—Garbage	**Nutter**—crazy person
Gutted—Devastated	**Knackered**—tired
Chuffed—Proud	**Gobsmacked**—amazed
Sorted—Arranged	**Chap**—male or friend
Hoover—Vacuum	**Wazzock**—an idiot
Kip—Sleep or nap	**Honking**—vomiting
Dodgy—Suspicious	**Arse over tit**—Fall Over
Wonky—Not Right	**Dog's dinner**—A Mess
Plonker—Idiot	**Toff**—Upper Class Person

I felt so sorry for him, but later on I gather he also saw the funny side of it, well he had to didn't he if he was going to be accepted into this unique force of men. The initiation over it was soon forgotten as the next victim joined the station. Whether or not the officer ever forgot, I doubt it, he just learnt the hard way, never tell the shift what you want to keep secret! I learn that lesson early on after seeing that and made sure that my fear of the dark was never revealed.

Many nights you found yourself at a hospital bed taking a statement from a witness or a victim, or sitting waiting for hours in casualty whilst waiting for a prisoner to be stitched up and released and given the all clear so that he could be charged for some offence that had happened earlier. Most disputes at night either came after a bar fight or a domestic fight, sometimes a combination of the two.

Once such fight was between a couple of young lovers who had a falling out. When one woman went back to her house she found her partner in bed with another woman and the sparks flew. It was a cat fight with spitting and scratching and biting, nothing like a typical male brawl. In fact, most officers, both male and female would say hat they rather deal with a male fight then a female one. On this occasion, the police were called and the one who broke into the house and was attacking the other two was takes away in the van.

She was going to be charged with the lesser charge of disturbing the peace, but there was no consoling her.

She had lost the love of her life to another woman and she was going to make everyone suffer, including me. I made the mistake of turning my back on her and within a second she had jumped on my back wrapping her arms around my neck and her legs around my thighs, causing me to fall forwards. She was attacking me, gesticulating like a dog. It took three other officers to pull her off of me. I wasn't seriously hurt, just bruised and scratched, but it taught me never to turn your back on anyone.

Because she was not calming down she could not be released for fear of what she was likely to go and do at the house in question. So it was decided to take her to a holding cell where there was a matron on duty that could watch her in the cells. As we loaded into the van, she continually tried to touch me, stroke me and call out lude obscenities. She had now focused her attention on me big time and it was necessary for a male officer to come with us to escort me escorting her. As we sat in the back, with him sitting between us, it was the longest ten minutes of my life.

CHAPTER SEVEN
COURT DUTY/DIVORCE COURT

Courts vary in size and types. The majority of cases that appear in the court will start in the Magistrates Court of which there are many in the London area and normally cases would appear in the Court covering the area that the offense was committed in.

The more serious criminal cases are tried on the basis of a document called the indictment.

The defendant is indicted on criminal charges specified in the indictment by the prosecutor. In most cases, the prosecution is on behalf of the Crown (the State) and is handled by an official agency called the Crown Prosecution Service, which takes the case over from the police who have already investigated most of the evidence.

The first stage will be to decide whether there is a case to answer what is called *a prima facie* case. This process, called committal, will be dealt with by a magistrate on the basis of evidence disclosed in papers provided by the prosecutor. If the case proceeds, it is heard in the Crown Court (there is only one Crown Court, but it has about 70 centers around the jurisdiction).

The trial is before a judge and jury. The judge presides over the trial process by attempting to ensure clarity and fairness. The judge must also consider and decide on legal issues such as whether a piece of evidence is admissible (should be put before the jury) and also instruct the jury as to the correct view of the law relevant to the case. The jury decides the facts (whose story is more believable) and applies the law to those facts. Therefore, it is the jury, not the judge, that reaches a verdict on the guilt or innocence of the defendant. In criminal cases, the prosecution has the burden of proof-it must prove guilt, rather than the defendant having to prove innocence. The standard of proof is heavy-guilt must be proven beyond reasonable doubt.

In less serious criminal cases which comprise over 90% of criminal cases, the case is sent for summary trial in one of over 400 Magistrates' Courts.

A summary trial means there is no committal and no jury. The trial is before a bench of magistrates. In most cases, there are three magistrates who are "lay" persons in other words, they are not professional judges nor are they lawyers, but, like the jury, they are persons from the local community. However, there are now an increasing number of stipendiary magistrates, which are paid magistrates who are qualified lawyers. Stipendiary magistrates are, for historical reasons, most common in London and in other large cities.

Those defendants who are dissatisfied by the verdict may be able to appeal:

1.1. from the Magistrates' Courts, there is an appeal to the Crown Court on matters of fact or law.

2.2. from the Crown Court, it might be possible to appeal to the Criminal

Division of the Court of Appeal on matters of fact or law

3.3. Certain legal disputes arising in the Magistrates courts or the Crown

Court can be taken before the Divisional Court of the High Court

Finally, matters of important legal dispute arising in the Crown Court or Divisional Court may be appealed to the House of Lords.

Civil Cases

In civil cases, the litigation is commenced by a plaintiff (a private person or company or a public authority) against a defendant. The plaintiff must try to prove the liability of the defendant on the balance of probabilities. The sorts of claims arising in the civil courts are typically about contracts (most common of all), torts (civil wrongs such as the causing a road accident through negligence, damaging a person's reputation through defamation, or affecting the enjoyment of their property through causing a nuisance such as by pollution) and land disputes. The choice of court depends in most cases on the value of the claim.

Claims of lesser value will start in a County Court. There are 250 County Courts around the country. They can also deal with divorce and bankruptcy matters. Relatively small claims (less than about £3,000) can be handled by a Small Claims Procedure.

This involves a quick hearing, often without lawyers being present, before a District Judge. The parties can, however, appeal to a Circuit Judge who also deals with full County Court trials. In 1995, nearly 2.5 million "actions" (cases) were commenced. Just over two million were actions for the recovery of debts based on contracts. Almost 200,000 were actions relating to land (mainly for repossession of houses where a mortgage or rent had not been paid). Another 200,000 related to matrimonial proceedings. The Small Claims Procedure dealt with 100,000.

More substantial civil claims (over around £25,000) are heard in the High Court (based in London but also with a few regional centres, often housed within Crown Court buildings). The action is begun by writ, which is accompanied by a statement of claim in which the details of the legal dispute is set out.

The High Court is organized according to case type into Divisions:

A Family Division deals with divorce and child welfare matters and also the administration of wills. Child welfare matters include both proceedings brought by child protection agencies, such as local authorities - about 17,000 in 1995. Parents and guardians may also make applications, for example about custody and access which included another 102,000 in 1995. There were also over 5,000 adoption orders.

Divorce is mainly dealt with in the County Courts, but the High Court does hear a small number of complex, contested cases.

The Family Division also oversees the uncontested administration of wills, a process called "probate". It authorizes the executors to act on behalf of the deceased person if it can be shown that all the papers are in order. There were about a quarter of a million grants of probate in 1995.

A Chancery Division considers complex matters such as disputes about wills, settlements and trusts, bankruptcy, land law, intellectual property (copyright and patents), and corporate laws. In 1995, nearly 11,000 general actions (mainly relating to land disputes) were begun. There were also 13,000 bankruptcy petitions and nearly 18,000 company cases (mainly relating to insolvency). Many of the company cases are dealt with in a specialist sub-Division, the Companies Court.

The Queen's Bench Division deals with the remaining business-disputes about contracts or torts or land. The Queen's Bench Division has some specialist sub-Divisions, including a Commercial Court (dealing with large and complex business disputes; there were about 200 in 1995), a Crown Office List (dealing with actions against public authorities, about 4,000), and an Admiralty Court (shipping matters about 500)

As you can see the British legal system has a wide variety of courts and the numbers of cases passing through them is ever growing. The staffing of which is vast and is required in all depts. Just to keep the system running efficiently.

Most Courts will have police officers on duty. Some are based there on a permanent posting and working in the office arranging the lists and organizing the requests for warrants issued when a defendant fails to attend court or answer to bail requirements that the court imposed on him.

They also are responsible for prisoners in the cells that have been brought over from Police Stations that have been charged with no bail, also those that are surrendering to bail and also prisoners already serving a sentence that are answering further charges and have been scheduled to appear in Court.

There are also witnesses, both civil and police that have to answer to maybe a request to attend court or a subpoena to attend.

Quite often when officers went on holiday or were sick they would request for a temporary posting from division for an officer to fill that position, thereby requiring our attendance at court for a set period.

Personally, I had very few postings to the courts, thankfully, as this was a specific posting that you either loved or hated. Somewhere it was decided that Divorce Court would be a place that a Policewoman's presence was necessary. What a depressing posting that turned out to be. In our area the Court sat once a week and I was required to be in attendance. Every time I came away after a day at that court I was convinced that I would never marry!

Mostly there would be couples arguing in front of a judge their own agenda and the reasons why they should have custody of the children, dog, or home. Both of them breaking down in tears would be the norm and at the end of each appearance I would be responsible for comforting them. I didn't have a lot of understanding of what they were going through as being single, and happy, these problems seemed somewhat self-inflicted. It wasn't until I myself went through an unpleasant divorce involving courts and solicitors that I saw it through different eyes.

A more interesting attachment would be the security duties that we were required to perform at some of the more high-profile cases.

The most high-profile case I was assigned to was one that involved the prosecutions resulting in the IRA bombings in London. The defendants were being tried in Winchester Crown Court and we were brought into the suburbs to add to the massive security programme that was set in place for this case.

The obvious risks were from Irish terrorists that might attack the court during the trial so we spent the whole time that the case was before the court traveling to the court and searching all attendees to the public seating. There were many family members of the accused and the security was at its highest.

Once everyone was searched and seated then we would sit at the back of the court and listen to the case at it was presented. Every time anyone left or entered the courtroom, we would have to check that they were not bringing something back into the courtroom that would cause an issue.

If you have never been to the courtrooms in Winchester, then they are well worth a visit. The main courtroom has the legendry "King Arthur's Round Table as a backdrop to the judges seating. Most impressive, and if it hadn't been that we were trying a horrific crime of multiple murder, then the moment would have been quite memorable.

The difference between the UK and USA Court system is quite vast. Sitting in the front row would be the prosecuting barrister representing the Crown and the defending barrister. Behind them would be the Solicitors and staff of the Inn that the Barristers are attached to. The Barristers are regaled in gowns and white wigs all hand woven and making an impressive appearance which is typical of all the Crown and High Courts. The magistrate's court and lesser courts would have solicitors representing their clients but dressed in regular business suits.

The UK law system, especially in the Crown Courts, is regaled in tradition and English customs. The overall look of the inside of a court when in progress is though it has travelled back in time, all members of the Bar wearing the same gowns and wigs having been worn for centuries, not literally I might add. Whereas he US system appears more casual with everyday suits and dresses being worn.

Whether you are appearing before a magistrates or a higher court, all witnesses are required to place their hand on the bible and swear in. They would claim that everything they said was the truth the whole truth and nothing but the truth so helps them god. Of course, those that did not believe in god or had another religion, would swear a different oath.

Our system, like others, is not perfect and over the years I saw cases being thrown out on a technicality or when evidence critical to the case was disallowed. Some because a doubt was put into the minds of the jury or judge that this case could not be 100% proven.

Sometimes a case could be lost over something very small but, provided the defense with a way their client could be found innocent. I often thought then that it was a very hard job to represent a client that you knew had committed the crime but as their legal representative it was your legal duty to represent them to the best of your ability. Personally, I couldn't have done that especially when serious sex crimes against women or children were involved. I often looked at that solicitor or barrister and wondered how they slept at night knowing that could be responsible in getting someone freed who should be inside only to allow them to re-offend. Such is the system, and an officer job stopped once you succeeded in getting to court and giving evidence.

It was then down to the court system and hopefully the correct decision would be made. One of the most frustrating points of law that I found time and time again was that you could not mention in evidence any priors that the defendant might have, even if he had previous records for the same offence.

I agree that the past conviction do not make a person guilty, but when a man has perhaps had four to five convictions of rape, indecent assault then when he is appearing yet again for the same offence with the same method of attack, then it has a bearing on the case. It shows he has done the same thing before and most importantly is capable of committing this type of crime.

I saw one case thrown out of court because we couldn't use past history of offences and we could not prove the case conclusively.

He was a worker with a TV repair company and was called into fix the TV. Most housewives when they have workers in their home would automatically offer them a drink of tea or coffee. It is a hospitality thing. In this case the woman was mid-thirties, attractive, and married. Whilst he worked, she chatted to him and they had a general conversation about everyday things. She laughed at his jokes and after about one hour as he was about to leave, he made a grab at her as she passed him. He pulled her to the ground, telling her that he knew she wanted him despite her cries for help and telling him to stop. He raped her and abused her for over two hours. Afterwards, he calmly picked up his tools, and left in his works van.

The victim was bruised and sore and felt dirty. Her first thought was to wash this man out of her body, his sperm, his smell, everything. Of course, that, evidence wise, is the worst that you can ever do, removing all evidence of bodily fluids that could perhaps be matched with the attacker. She rang the police and told them she had been raped and of course the system kicked in.

However, passing over the next few weeks of the case, when it came to court, the defense claimed that because she had given him a drink and had spent time talking and joking with him that he had read that to mean that she was giving him the come on. Basically, he claimed that he believed that she was flirting with him and that she wanted to have sex with him. He claimed that he cry's for help and her insistence that he should stop was all part of the game. Basically, the defense put a small amount of doubt in the minds of the jury and he was found not guilty.

That poor woman had to live with the shame that the case levied against her. Her husband felt she had put herself at risk by being friendly and now she had the stigma of being a liar and easy to boot. She regretted ever taking the case to court and even though he had previous in his history this could not be used. Is that fair? I leave it for you to decide....

CHAPTER EIGHT
...A4... Scotland Yard

I was well settled into my station by now and out of my probation period, I had passed my final exams with flying colours with good marks. Now, I was ready for more responsibility and they allocated me my own station.

It was not totally my own of course, but I was the only Policewoman there, so I could plan my own shifts and as long as we had cover over the district, then I could plan my own working week.

The station I was at was very close to Elstree Studios and was on my beat so quite often when returning to the station I would pop into see who or what was happening on set. It was amazing to see the sets as they were built, and even more amazing to see the artists as they prepared to go onto the set. Some of them that I imagined to be as beautiful off set as they were on greatly shocked me. They were bordering on plain, sitting there with rollers in their hair, no make-up and a fag hanging out the side of their mouth.

It was quite an eye-opener. In fact, on one occasion myself and another officer were standing watching a scene where two robbers were clamouring out of the window when the producer yelled us at for not being where we should be. We looked at each other quizzically and then realized that he had in fact mistaken us for the actors who were dressed as police officers and due to be in the scene. It wasn't until the two fake officers burst through the window in hot pursuit that he realized his mistake… it caused a number of giggles in the filming crew I can say. That was the first and last time that I was ever mistaken for a film star in uniform!

I was enjoying myself immensely at my new station when the call came that every WPC dreaded. Every 6 months divisions had to supply two officers to man the department in New Scotland Yard which dealt with prostitutes, dead bodies, and missing children.

The only good thing about it was that my then husband, who was stationed on A division, could give me a lift, if we were ever on the same shift, which wasn't that often.

It meant long days, as the shift would start at 5:45 a.m. and that would mean catching the first bus at 4:30am to the train station and then one of the first trains into the centre of London.

That was a horrible shift, getting up so early meant that you either had to go to bed so early you couldn't go out or have a social life, or you would get very little sleep. Whichever way it didn't do much for your private life. Late duty wasn't much better as starting at two p.m. meant you finished at ten p.m. and got you home too late to do anything other than go to bed. Of course, nights meant so going out at all at night and sleeping all day, if you weren't disturbed that is.

I have to admit that initially I was very upset at being moved from my station, which I had only just settled into, and being put onto a department that I had no interest in or desire to work in.

However, if I have learnt anything working in the police, is never to pre-judge. Not long after working there I started to find a fascination in the work that we were involved in. The challenges were different each day.

The department itself was set up to deal with missing persons, dead bodies and prostitutes. Sometimes of course, the three could be one of the same. The work involved hours of searching through files as long as the eye could see. At that time, we didn't have the luxury of computers. Every call that came in had to be collated and put in a file.

Every possible piece of information would be gathered regarding description of the person missing, birthmarks, scars, colour of eyes, hair, nicknames, strange habits or dress, anything that could be a vital piece of information. Some of these missing persons were teenage runaways that would head for London looking for excitement and end up walking around homeless in the Piccadilly area or any other area of London they happen to run out of money in. Some people wouldn't want to be found and would disappear leaving no trace.

The children, those being under the age of 18years, were of prime concern to the police as many would be at risk once reaching London. They became the prey of pimps looking for new fresh flesh to supply to their customers or to the perverts that wandered the streets and public conveniences looking for a tired, lost, and frightened child who came to London for excitement and realising that there was nowhere to go, would accept a 'friendly face who offered them a bed for the night. I shudder each time I think of the many children who have gone down that route and have never been seen again. Some to be found in gruesome circumstances, some to never be found.

Of course, when a person is picked up and taken into a station in London they would be asked various questions to help identify them. Sometimes, they were so tired and desperate to return home they would give their details willingly, some that were less eager to return home for whatever reason would make it very difficult. Sometimes they would give a false name and address. It was then left to the officer dealing to be very precise in the details be observed. Accent was a giveaway and date of birth. Although they gave it and changed the year, normally they kept the month and day, which of course we could check against our registers.

Once the officer obtained as much info as possible then it was our turn to start going through the files. We would check the name first and normally that would be false. So we would go through everything. For example, all the blondes, aged about 14-years with blue eyes and a scar on left elbow with a nose stud and a Liverpool accent. If all the correct info was given at the time of the person going missing, then by elimination of all other details we could narrow it down. Sometimes, it was easy, and sometimes it took hours ending with two or three possibilities.

Of course, when you confronted them with the name normally they would be so surprised that we managed to trace them that they would then give in and admit their true identity. We then started the job of re-uniting them with their families.

The families that genuinely missed their child were only too pleased to come and get them. Some were not so keen. Maybe the family circumstances were so bad they left to get away from constant beatings or a stepfather who was coming into her bedroom and making suggestions of how he could show her "real" love. So many sad cases and of course if that became the case then it would then involve Social Services to come and ascertain what the circumstances were and whether they could intervene.

Some, once returned, would run off the next day back to London or another big city, only this time they got a little wiser as to what to ay or not say, to hide their identity.

Some would be encouraged to work the streets to earn a living, a percentage of which they paid to their pimp who was now going to look after them.

Of course, the majority of these men would get into the affections of the women and get them dependant on them emotionally then blackmail them into working for them. The girls that became part of that life found it very difficult to leave. They would be beaten badly if they did not give up the high percentage of takings that was demanded so there was very little chance of them finding a better way to live.

As a rule, there was a very strong bond between these girls, there had to be. Society has always been aware that ladies of the night existed, but it was not something they wanted to see or be reminded of. It has been a profession supplying a service to a group in society that had the need to find women willing to participate in either sex or some other service they could not find at home or elsewhere.

They say it is one of the oldest professions in the world and in many countries it is accepted as a normal way of life. So much so that there are special Red Light districts set up where they can legally trade in safety and get regular health checks reducing risk to them and their clients.

Of course, the red light was used for a purpose, you normally find that a red light has a complimentary reflection on old and tired skin so the redder the light the older the woman. Quite often the young fresh women who hadn't yet gained the benefits of age would use lighter coloured bulbs. The men dressed as women nearly always had a red light to hide any obvious signs of masculinity.

Of course, England has never in society been tolerant of this profession, which keeps the profession as illegal. It was quite amusing to see them hanging out of the windows, their breasts barely covered resting on the sill, legs akimbo on stair wells offering services to those passing by.

When the call went out that a "Rozzer" was coming the windows were shut quickly, legs and breasts disappeared quicker than you could say Friar Tuck. As soon as they turned the corner windows were opened and the limbs and parts of the body free were hoisted up into view once again. This was the occurrence in numerous of the central streets of London, some areas worse than others. Of course at night they ventured out more and gathered on street corners. At this stage it was harder for them to run and hide and they had to then use a different means of avoiding reporting.

At that time, in law, a prostitute once having been seen and heard to be offering sex for money would be allowed three cautions before she could be arrested and charged. So there stated the game. The officer would write down her details and give as good a description he could and call us up with the details. If we had no other report matching those details, then we would register Warning one.

The next time she was caught and the report made she would have got to Warning two and so on until she made the third. Then she would be arrested and taken to the station, charged, and bailed to appear at court in the morning. Mainly on appearance it would be a fine. By most, this would be deemed as their "tax" on their earnings.

However, some of them were very canny when it came to being caught. Once they had had their warning they would rush off back to their flat or place of business and change clothes, wig, glasses or lenses to another colour, height of shoe and anything else that could identify them. So, the next time they were caught the description would not tie up with the last one so she would remain at only 1 caution. This could go on for week after week until she duplicated or an officer would twig who she really was. Even the accent would change.

It was amazing at the tricks that they would come up with. Sometimes the officer would not be observant and give a totally different description from his colleague who stopped them ten minutes earlier. That really confused things. Especially when it was a matter of height or weight, you wouldn't believe the variance in such a short space of time. It was amazing how a person can shrink by six inches and put on five stone. We had quite a few laughs when we matched them by date of birth. We didn't let the officer forget it either!

Again, every report that came in got filed in descriptions that had to be refined and listed individually so that everything could be cross-referenced. There was a card in each of the files so that if we had no name we would do it by height or eyes or scars. Anything that was visible was noted.

If any of these ladies of the night turned up as a dead body then we could normally find them as nearly all their details would be noted and although time consuming, at least we were able to tie up the loose ends and ascertain who she was.

As well as being in charge of these three sections for Scotland Yard, we were also responsible for accepting the first call for a major disaster, warning the senior officer and calling in all those on call.

I was on duty when the first major disaster came in reporting the Airplane crash in Tenerife in the 1970's that had a full loss of life. Within minutes the room, which had numerous phone lines and computers, was activated and all staff called in to man the phones.

The night remember was a Sunday and had to phone my Chief superintendent who was at home having dinner. She rushed back in and took command of the situation, which was a grim task to do. So many frantic calls from family members ringing to find out if their loved ones were on the flight and whether they had survived. Unfortunately, all perished and the task of identification must have been a horrendous task for those dealing with it.

Anything that happens on such a large scale causes a lot of discussion and upset so it was not surprising that when the same chief superintendent left on the Friday evening and told me that she didn't want a repeat of last Sunday, that when got the call to tell me that another plane crash had happened exactly one week later only this time at Heathrow, she didn't believe me at first. The odds of a repeat accident with total loss on two successive Sundays are almost beyond belief, yet it happened and again had to set everything up. This time it was worse as the local police had to deal with sightseers who always at had accidents turn up to see the gruesome sights. Of course, this didn't help services get to the site and delayed things and blocked the road.

Fortunately, that was the end of the disasters whilst did my term of duty up there and eventually, the time I was assigned to the department came to an end. I didn't miss the early mornings or late nights but I did miss the challenges that we faced daily.

There was nothing more rewarding in having to look through files to find the person who was sitting the other side of London saying nothing, and supply the station with the information of that person. Maybe somewhere along the line by doing a thorough job I maybe helped someone to get back to their loving family and away from all the risks and dangers they would have been exposed to if they hadn't been found by an officer.

Sometimes during day shifts if we were quiet, we would be encouraged to go to records and see how massive the system was and how it worked. In today's world of computerization this system would be used but it was fascinating to see how everything linked, not only in the UK, but also around the world in other Police systems and Interpol.

My sergeant in that department was an older, robust officer who never married and made the police force her whole life. She was a great inspiration and a great character that enjoyed working with. She definitely made the less interesting moments in A4 worthwhile

It was amazing that she could have been a double for the actress Margaret Rutherford, for which she was always being teased by her "girls" We used to tell her that she was really an actress on the side and was working in A4 as a sideline. That always put a smile on her face.

I believe she passed away a few years ago after retiring from the force. I had enjoyed my time there more than had ever expected to and was grateful for the experience. She taught me a lot about the art of filing and cross filing. It probably held me in good stead for all the paperwork that this job constantly produced.

My assignment over, now it was time for me to return to my station and to start to get myself a routine in place. The thought of working my own schedules out with the duty sergeant was something was looking forward to, as now I only had to be answerable to him and not the WPS that ran the team of WPC's at the main station.

I would pretty much be able to plan my working week around jobs and court cases and of course married life, which now might be able to take a place in the rest of my responsibilities.

CHAPTER NINE
Borehamwood

When I was given my posting after my 2 yrs. probation, I was delighted to be offered Borehamwood and Elstree. Of course, I didn't have much time to get settled before I was whisked off to A4 at Scotland Yard. Now I was back, and I could get myself settled into a routine.

When a new WPC arrives at a station there is always little interest by the wives of the officers that you will be working with. Most of the wives want to know that their husbands are going to be spending an 8-hour sight shift with another woman who they can trust. I was quite aware of how they might regard me with a little suspicion, so I made sure that right from the start I got to meet most of them at the Police Club as soon as I could. The best way of getting their trust was to become their friend and made great efforts to meet as many wives as I could so that they were confident that would take care of their husbands opposed to flirt with them or worse.

Having said that, the reverse actually proved to be the case. One night shift, one of the younger single officers asked if I wanted to go on patrol with him. WPC's were not allowed to go out on their own at night for security reasons and so we normally paired up with another officer. Having booked the car out and our radios, we headed out on patrol. I was under the impression that we were heading in one direction when after a short while I noticed that we were driving further and further into the more rural part of the division. I asked about this and he said that he wanted to check on a house that he had been asked to look after. I believed his, why wouldn't I? He was fellow officer and you expect to trust each other.

We eventually pulled over in what appeared to be dense woodland. When I enquired obviously where the property was, it was quite clear that there was no property. In fact, he obviously thought that being out with a young WPC gave him the right to take advantage of the night shift, and the fact that we were out alone where we would not be seen.

He started to make advances to me telling me that I obviously I wanted him. In fact, according to him, most women did, and most policewomen certainly were easy so what was I complaining about. I felt quite sick with a real feeling of fear in the pit of my stomach. Here I was in a very precarious position, which in normal circumstances I would never have found myself in. I would never have got into a stranger car, who I hardly know, and allowed myself to be driven to an unknown destination without knowing where I was going.

I had all these thoughts going through my head, was be seriously expecting me to allow him to do what he wanted? I came out with a fellow officer, someone who you should be able to trust, not someone who is threatening you with sexual advances. For a few moments I had a slight feeling of panic, but then thought that this is perhaps what he was counting on. Somehow, had to convince him that this was not a good idea and that perhaps if joked with him could deter him from going any further with this. I was getting the vibe that be felt that it was important to him to have control and rape is a matter of control. Nothing to do with sexual intimacy. Just the ability to be able to control the woman.

If he had sex on his mind, then it was my intention to get it off his mind. I didn't want to get into the position where I challenged him and it turned nasty. So, I tried talking him down, telling him he shouldn't think that every policewoman was looking for a man and certainly he shouldn't think that because I was with him out in the wilds it was because I was looking for sex in the back of a panda car. I tried the tact of telling him that I was ig (married) and that I was flattered, but I would decline the offer.

I joked with him and changed the subject continually until the scent eased. I wanted to take away the tension and without making him feel threatened. If he had laid one finger on me, then I would have fought like a wildcat and done some damage to him. However, I didn't want to end up as a victim that fought back, but was overcome and then end up on a witness stand having to give evidence against a fellow officer and have my reputation pulled through the mud. I have seen so many rape cases where the woman did nothing, but the defense would claim that she gave the green light by smiling or joking.

After a time had passed, I commented that we had better report in otherwise they might wonder where we are and immediately called the station to see if there was anything needed to be done. I told them we were turning back to the station. At that, he seemed to pull himself back to reality and he started the car back up and headed back to the station. He obviously started to think about what he had done, and or nearly done and started to get a little concerned. He asked if I was going to say anything and that he didn't mean anything by it, he was just trying his luck. He was sorry and hoped that I wasn't upset by it.

Upset by it, of course I was upset, I had been rather unnerved by the whole incident. Having said that, this officer was not stupid, and I could see that he was working out what he would say, should I complain. I could see that he would turn the tables and say that I came on to him. So, at that point, I decided that this matter would stay between the two of us. If I reported him, I could lose a lot of respect from other officers, and if the wives believed it had been me making a move on him then my time at the station would come to an end.

Amazing as it may seem, in those days, women were at a great disadvantage in the force, there were so many male officers in ranking positions that would welcome the chance to make a WPC look bad. So, I kept quiet. I hated having to do that, but I had no physical damage, just a very unpleasant experience. I was the only women officer at the station so, there was no other WPC at this station he could take out and I could make sure that none of the other of my fellow female officers went out with him. I would never go with him, again, and I always made sure that I went out with other officers before he could ask me to go with him. I think a couple of the other officers guessed what had happened, and they were great. They knew that this officer was, in fact, not as honest as he should be, and he was suspected of doing things that were not legal. I later heard that he had been involved in some burglary thefts and had been charged and was sentenced to a prison term. It couldn't have happened to a better person.

When it came round to Christmas, I was roped into helping with organizing the children's party; that was so much fun. I booked the location, which was the officers club, and then got some of my fellow female officers to join in. We went along to Elstree studios and asked if they would allow us to use some of their costumes for the party. They were great and gave us the key to the wardrobe! I couldn't believe it, the whole of the studio at our pleasure. We went along to look at what was there, and it was mind blowing. So much to choose from, but what attracted us the most was the Dr. Who set of clothes. We found some really great outfits, silver metallic with wigs and all the trimmings we needed to make us look like star travellers. The party was a complete success, and of course, it was a great way to get to know all the wives and their children. I was now totally accepted into the family of the station.

There were some great characters at this station, both young and old, some new on division and some at the end of their career. Some were a little crazy; in fact, you never knew what one officer would do next. He had been known to walk into the front office with a parrot on his shoulder doing a pirate accent, another time he would hang upside down over the front desk and one occasion a member of the public came in and rang the hell whereby he lowered himself down and said to the person standing there that he was just hanging about and would be back soon, with that he lifted himself back up and disappeared out of view of this person. How on earth do you deal with that? On this occasion just had to deal with the person's query, and pretend that nothing abnormal had just happened. God knows what that person must have thought and would have said when getting home. As for us well, we would have fallen about the station laughing but at the time it was all we could do to keep a straight face.

One of the perks at night was that we had the key to the swimming pool across from the station and when we checked it out we used to take a swim. There is nothing like taking a late night swim at two a.m. with just the moon for light in a full sized pool. Fortunately, we never got a call whilst we had our little dip, otherwise it might have been embarrassing to have turned up with wet hair and improperly dressed.

We had great bakers on the beat that would start baking their bread for the day at about five a.m. We all went round just before booking off to collect our bread to take home. Hot and fresh, ready to take a big chunk of butter, a hot drink, then a nice cozy bed to get your sleep before starting another shift.

Injuries are part and part of the job, but sometimes if you are not careful, it is not the criminal that inflicts it. On this particular shift I was out with the area car on patrol which meant you got a lot of the emergency calls. The area car was a Jaguar, which was one of the models they used to use in the 60's. Whilst out on a shout (a call for help), we had to go to a junkyard to investigate a complaint. We had no sooner got out of the car and started toward the caravan (officer when the guard dog, a very large Alsatian Dog shot out of the caravan. He was barking ferociously, and the teeth were very evident. It didn't look as though he was coming out to welcome us.

The driver of the vehicle yelled to all of us to get back in the car and we all turned and ran. Unfortunately, part of our uniform included skirts, which were pencil in design, and didn't give you the ability to actively, jump in and out of cars gracefully. I got to the car door, managed to get it open and jumped in. I was so concerned about getting my legs in before the dog got to them, that as I got my legs in, I pulled the door shut. I forgot how shallow the back door was in the Jaguar. As I ducked in, I didn't duck enough so as I shut the door my head hit the car frame, then the door shut on my head...now that looked funny believe me and although I managed to get my head in, it had a nasty bump on it. The laughs that went around the car dented my pride as well. Of course, the station had it regaled to them, time and time again.

We're not busy, On Night duty Policewomen on outer divisions covered not only their own division but also covered the two closest. So, I was on S, but I also covered Q and Y. there was only one of us on, so believe me, it was rare that you ever stayed at your own station. You never got to work on your own territory very often. Nearly every night when you arrived, there would be a call waiting for you to ring a station needing a WPC.

One evening, on arrival I was told that a station on Y had need of me. They were sending a car for me so expect to leave promptly. The car arrived, as promised, and as we left, I asked what the problem was. I was told it was a female problem, no kidding Sherlock that was no surprise. It didn't matter what I said, they were not going to tell me; all they would say that I would find out when I arrived.

As I walked in, the station officer explained that a female had been brought in for disturbing the peace and that she had been "difficult". All the officers were huddled in the corner, one holding his head with a towel, another looking dishevelled and waiting for me to go into the charge room. What on earth could be so terrible that no one wonted tells me. What on earth had happened? As I went into the charge room I saw a broken table, a smashed chair, items scattered all over the floor and a female standing stark naked. She had a chair leg in one hand, a stiletto heel in the other and was swearing and cursing at me as I stood there totally unprepared for what was about to deal with.

She had obviously had been responsible for the damage to both the items in the room and the officers that were holding their injuries outside. Of course, she had stripped off knowing full well that most male officers would now back off what does a male officer grab hold of without being accused of sexual assault? Now, I know why I was brought in. I had to get her into the cell without getting my head caved in or worse. Well, size wise I was about 5'6" and weighed about 10st, while this female was about 5'10" and weighed in about 14st. Not only did she outweigh me she had two weapons and I had none.

I thought that this was definitely a time for psychology. She did not know me and what I was or wasn't capable of. I was not keen to start hand to hand combat especially as she held all the weapons so decided that the best way forward was to bluff my way out of it. I suggested, using her own terminology, that if she didn't put down the weapons immediately, I would be placing them where the sun didn't shine. I was shaking inside, but I took on a hard attitude hoping that she believed me.

If it didn't work, and she attacked me, then I would have called for extra assistance and tried to disarm her. She stood there for a few minutes, glowering at me and sweating profusely but I could see whether or not she could win in this situation. She decided that dropping the weapons were her best way forward, which she did and sat back down. At that point, the men who had been watching behind the door came in and assisted me getting her into a cell. Once in and door shut, I think she realized that she had been duped and then spent the next couple of hours banging on the door and calling me all the names she could think of. Eventually the drink took its toll and she curled up on the bed and wrapped herself in the blanket and slept it off!

No sooner had that situation been dealt with but another call came through that was needed in Holloway were a woman had committed suicide by jumping from a high bridge. I had to report to the hospital, and help ascertain her identity, collect possessions and then inform any relatives we could find. This was going to be a busy night, one of many in my three week set of night duties.

Fortunately, some nights were quiet, and although it dragged somewhat, it at least gave me the opportunity of catch up with paperwork. And believe me, there was plenty of that. We had to keep notebooks and write report of everything we did. All of our reports on arrests, cautions, and time on patrol had to be noted and those that we were on patrol with, in case we needed to verify anything. You have to remember, if anything we were involved with went to court then we had to be able to confirm and recollect the events that happened. Bearing in mind that sometimes it took months for a case to be heard in court and it was impossible to remember everything that happened. So, we were allowed to take our notebooks or any statements we made into court to help refresh our memories. It was important that we wrote every little detail down that might be questioned or disputed.

When we took our breaks we also had use of a snooker/pooltable, which was in our rest area, and helped us relax before heading out on our next call. In the 60's and 70's, police stations were open 24 hours, so even though we might be on break, we never knew when we would be needed.

CHAPTER TEN
Underground

This part of police work offered a variety of interesting, yet sometime risky, duties depending on the department that you were attached to.

Serious Crimes unit, Drugs unit, Home Office unit and Escort Duties were some of the units that I was assigned to work in over my years in the service.

Some officers looked like an officer in and out of uniform some did not. When I let my hair down and dressed in civvies. I looked far from a police officer so that gave me a lot of opportunity to participate in various stings.

On one occasion, I was told to report to a certain station and listen to the detective inspector run through the events planned for the evening. Thoughts passed through my mind about why on earth would I want to walk alone through a dark lonely street, wearing a short skirt and a skimpy jacket. No weapons, no truncheon, just a whistle, which I was going to hold close to my lips.

As the information came out, I found out I was going to be the bait to lure out a rapist who had been attacking young women who long blonde hair. I fit the bill. Of course, they tell you it's voluntary, but I was getting a little nervous. I didn't like the dark and a heavy fog was slowly settling in, but I joined the force to help people, and if by my help we caught the man doing this, I might prevent another woman from being attacked.

I was trying to build up my confidence when the Inspector looked at me and told me that my skirt wasn't short enough, and I was wearing tights not stockings… really? I didn't know how to respond with a room full of men waiting for my response, so I took a deep breath and replied, "With respect sir, if you want someone to make it easy by wearing stockings, I suggest you wear them! I'm quite prepared to go out on a dark foggy night but I'm going to make it a struggle for this man to get what he wants and to give you guys to get to me, sir!"

Well, fortunately, after a few moments of silence everyone burst out laughing. They saw the funny side of it, what they didn't see that underneath the tights were a tight pair of body huggers that took me 15 minutes to squeeze into, so his chance of getting them off quickly was zero. Trouble is, I needed notice if I needed to use the bathroom so I didn't drink the hot coffee being handed out, or I'd never be ready for the start of the Obs (observation).

In theory, the risk was minimal, the walk was to take had an officer walking ahead on the other side of the road, one inside a doorway, another walking a dog (of the police biting variety) and another one driving up and down. All this was to guarantee my safety, but the night was getting very foggy and the distance that one could see anything was greatly being reduced by the second.

So, we all headed off into the night, everyone was aware of what to do in the event of an attack. However, because of the lack of vision now it very much relied on my ability to be able to scream or blow my whistle and if he was to approach from behind and knock me down, then there was little chance of being seen.

At this moment in time I just wonder, why had taken this career move?

To do good? To help people? All good intentions and ideals, but in truth, at this very moment walking down this lane in total darkness and fog to boot wondered about my sanity...I was so scared.

I had my scarf pulled around my head, hiding my hand which had the police whistle ready at my lips. The order was that if anyone approached me or tried to grab me. I was to blow it for all was worth, God help the guy who was asking for directions! I was blowing it!!

What if they knocked my hand away? What if dropped the damn whistle? All this was going through my mind, what I wouldn't give for being at the disco with my friends or curled up in front of the TV watching a movie.

The night was getting colder and the fog worse. I had walked back and forth along this path about 12 times. Of course, I had to wear stiletto heels which didn't help the feet but they wanted me to look as typical of his previous victims.

After several hours it was decided that nothing was going to happen and we were called back to the station. The mobile officer picked me up and we all headed back to the station for a debriefing. Obviously, the rapist had other plans that night and a part of me was very grateful...

Serious Crimes Squad

Sometime later, I got a call to report to Scotland Yard where I was going to be attached to a squad and I was to dress smart casual. On arrival, I went into a large meeting room where a variety of people were sitting, bikers, tramps, hippies, drug addicts, what on earth had walked into? My jaw must have hit my chest as an officer informed me that these were all undercover officers and were being used in the sting taking place. I would never in a month of Sundays have recognized these people as officers...it was a real eye opener.

I certainly gained an admiration for those that took on a life where they slept on the streets and gave up their home life for sleeping under Tower Bridge. That was dedication.

This job was monitoring a gang of jewellery thieves

who had been breaking into large stores without being seen and emptying the vault during the night. So my job was to play the part of "the girlfriend of the Inspector" walking along the street looking at rings in the window, whilst at the same time seeing if we could see anything odd happening at the back of the store.

After we were all deployed and headed out to our positions, no one would have known the area was crawling with police, the old lady walking her dog, a biker hanging around with a group outside the café, nothing obvious.

We had received information that this evening they would be raiding one of the stores, unfortunately, we didn't know which one. They had been investigating this gang for months and all information received had to be verified reliable.

After a couple of hours, the inspector decided that it would be too obvious to continue, there's only so many times you can look in a window without seeming suspicious. So, we headed back for the debriefing and every officer would write down observations, including who they had seen in the area. It is well known that these criminals are professionals that have their own scouts out looking at the area, and if they see anything out of place or not right, then they would call off the job.

So, every time they set up one of these obs (observation), they have to change out the officers and the set up or their scouts would recognize them and then it is blown. I hadn't realized until then how much time and effort was put into catching some of the criminals that plan everything carefully. It can take years of policing to catch the gang. This night we weren't lucky.

Drugs

A lot of plain clothes work is done in an effort to catch those selling or using drugs. My next call was to be an insider at a party, and find out who was holding the drugs so that when the uniformed branch entered, they didn't have time to hide or destroy the drugs.

On arriving at this house in North London, the house was full of young people, dancing, drinking and having fun…just having a good time.

No one challenged us going in and we began to mingle in the room watching to see who was passing the drugs. It's not an easy task when everyone is crammed in and dancing and it was hard to keep an eye on hand movements without looking obvious and alerting a dealer you were there.

We watched carefully and knew the time the officers would arrive with the warrant at which time we would expect people to drop packets and/or run to the bathroom and flush them. At the exact time the door burst open and officers flooded in, and the packets started dropping, the girl closest to me dropped hers by my feet so I picked up and gave it back to her, "I think you dropped this", "thank you" was her reply at which point I arrested her for possession. For the next 10 minutes, people were rushing everywhere, and people were being arrested by the dozen.

The Police van filled quickly, and a large number of partygoers were taken back to the station where they were all charged for possession of an illegal substance. On this occasion we only caught the small fish, the dealer had come in earlier and cleared out before we could find him.

The sad thing is that so many of these kids accept it as part of having fun, and it gives them a kick until they need more and more of it, ending up as an addict then begins the downward path to degradation and possible death. In the 60' & 70's, the drugs available were different to what is on the streets now and the groups being targeted have grown from school kids to professionals. A sad side of society.

INDECENT BEHAVIOUR

Many of Britain's sex laws are from laws from a past era. The vagrancy Act of 1824 (since updated, covering more offenses) gave us the law required to prosecute "flashers" along with common law offenses of "outraging public decency"

Technically, someone needs to be outraged which of course was normally the case. The football fan that decided run around the pitch totally naked to celebrate the goal is treated as a public nuisance opposed to someone who is a sexual pervert.

Of course, this offense straddles many different types of variants, all under the act. (Sexual Offenses Act 2003) Most people think of this offense is just in relation to dirty old men exposing themselves, that is so far from the truth. It covers certain sections of prostitution and also now covers indecency acts towards children.

Men exposing themselves were always happening, and traditionally it seemed to be more reports when it was very cold or very hot. I don't know if there is statistical data to support, but it certainly was what I experienced.

In the past it was treated as the low end of the scale but studies have shown that 14% of child molesters and 20% of rapists have in their earlier years exposed themselves. So, although there was almost a certain humor and bad jokes made about the event it's actually not funny for the victim and potentially the beginning of more serious actions.

Being stationed in North London, it was close to many parks and open spaces and these seemed to be the favorite haunt of these offenders. Flashing was the terminology given to the offender and quite often they would hide in bushes and jump out to show themselves to a woman or child passing by.

I personally was flashed too, when I was 12 years old whilst playing in the park close to my home when that actually happened. I remember it as if it was yesterday, so it definitely was an event that registered.

I remember seeing a man in the bushes watching me and as I walked by, he called me over. I didn't go near him, as I sensed something was wrong, and turned to go home but not before I saw he was holding his penis in his hand and pointing to it.

I felt sick to my stomach and am still amazed how I can remember details so clearly. I really didn't understand what was happening, but I knew enough to be scared and I ran home to tell my mother. She immediately picked up a rolling pin and charged off toward the place it happened. Unfortunately, or fortunately he had gone but she had intended in doing him some damage.

When she returned, I asked her if she was going to call the police, but she said there was no point as he had gone. Now, knowing what I do that was a bad decision as if she had called it might have been one of many flashings in the area and officers would then have gone undercover which is how we find them.

Traditionally, men often would wear a raincoat and trousers that went from the knees to their ankles so from the waist to the knees they were naked so they would flash open the coat showing all they had. The offense needed for the penis to be erect or he was masturbating. If he could prove he was only urinating, then there was a chance he would get off, but you can't urinate if in a rigid state. So, the evidence the victim gave was very important and sometimes being shocked or upset they were not good witnesses.

Primarily, that is why they used officers to volunteer to be the "victim" as they were trained in observation skills and were more likely to ensure the offender was found guilty.

Sometimes, people take things into their own hands, as was the case one day near Hampstead Heath. We would get many calls to that area and I happened to be in the station getting ready to go undercover on the Heath.

So, whilst standing in the front office, a little old lady hobbled in with the assistance of a wobbly wooden walker stick with a large brass knob on the end. She was very irate and obviously upset. She kept repeating "I got the bleeder good; I got the dirty bleeder!"

Our first question was to ascertain if she was unhurt and once told she was we took her to the interview room.

Then the tale unravelled. She had gone out to the local phone box to call her daughter and whilst talking her noticed a man hovering about and assumed he was waiting to use the phone. She heard him knocking on the window impatiently and without turning round told him to "bugger off", a poplar expletive in the UK.

The knocking continued and she was getting annoyed, so she looked round and he was pointing downwards, she looked down to see him holding his large erect penis and knocking it against the window. She was incensed, and without pausing she dropped the phone, walked outside to where the man was standing and with one heavy swipe she swung her cane down and hit his penis and balls with the brass knob on her stick. Twice!

The man collapsed screaming on the floor, and with that she came to the office to report it. On hearing that, several officers ran to the phone box to find the man still curled up on the floor with blood everywhere and a very black and blue nether region.

An ambulance was called and he was taken to hospital and later charged and appeared in court.

Our little old lady, aged 81 years old, acted in self-defence in fear of being raped and she stood up and gave evidence like a pro.

The judges face was a picture; here was this little old lady who had stood up to this 25-year-old, strongly built guy and given him summary justice. (instant reprisal/justice on the spot).

I think the judge was close to chuckling, but made it clear that justice was swift, and just, and he sentenced him accordingly. He praised the bravery of the old lady who waived her stick yet again. "I'd do it again, my Lord, he was a dirty bugger". What a gem. I never forgot that lady, very brave. I doubt the offender would forget her either, he had the scars to look at in case he forgot!

I still find it amazing that some of these flashers when caught, said they did it to pick up women. When asked to explain he said that some women were offended, but some would come closer to look and then agree to a sexual act. I still am shocked at that, speechless honestly, and that takes a lot for those that know me. How low can women go and degrade herself, or am I looking at it the wrong way?

London Underground

This is a place where more common assaults happen than you can imagine, especially at rush hour. Whilst everyone is jammed in like sardines in the carriage, and can't get a seat, they try to hang on to a rail or grip, which means one hand holds their bag and the other in in the air holding onto supports, but unable move it down.

So, then, the man who feels he is in a position to assault a female would then move close enough to either masturbate against her, touch her lower area or breasts, and they are unable to move. Most women freeze and freak out as it happens so quickly, and as soon as the train pulls into the next station everyone moves in, out or along the carriage.

I spoke to a lady who reported it and said that it had happened to her on more than one occasion and she was getting tired or it. So, she found a way to stop it. "How did you do that?" I asked. She replied, "Very easily. I just shout at the top of my voice "Would the dirty pervert who is grabbing my arse!! and masturbating stop immediately" She said everyone turns round and all the men make an effort to move away. I burst out laughing. So ladies, if you are ever in that position, do the same… it works. Girl Power!

CHAPTER ELEVEN
Security Attachments

The Inner divisions used to get snowed under with all the dignitaries visiting Central London, which required extra manpower. So, if you were attached to an outer division, there was always the opportunity to work overtime.

The jobs were varied and each one held a different type of skill. During the late 60's and early 70's London regularly would have demonstrations at the weekend. Some groups would apply for permission to march, and therefore, we would know the route, where it would start and where it was due to end. We would know approximately how many would attend, who would be speaking and what problems might arise.

The first one I was involved in was in 1968, at the end of the year not long before graduating. At the time we were still in training in Hendon when the call was sent out. A march that was being held to protest the US presence in Vietnam was growing in numbers, far more than had been anticipated. Not only that, the crowd was getting angry with agitators amongst them causing violent outbursts. It was very clear that the number of officers that had been allocated to the march was vastly underestimated and more were needed.

The call went out to off duty officers, and they pulled in whomever they could muster. Reports were coming in that the angriest of the marchers were heading directly for the US Embassy, with the intention of breaking into the Embassy as a protest. The Embassy is legally US soil and anyone breaking in would be met with Marines, standing armed and ready to fire at any intruders breaking in.

By now, high-ranking officers were extremely concerned about the situation. If these demonstrators managed to get through the front line of officers, then the next thing to occur would be a blood bath, as getting through the Embassy would have been met with the full force of the Marines. As a last resort, they called for all the officers in the college to be brought out as extra support. WPC's were kept mainly in the prison van whilst the men were pushed into the front line. After much reorganizing and redirecting, the extra officers that were drafted in managed to stave off the marchers and peace was eventually restored.

It was a long day and I am sure every officer was tired and many of them bruised with the conflicts they had had to endure.

The next few months offered us the opportunity of extra money by working the demonstrations that took place every Sunday. You would arrive at a given point where you would receive your instructions and which bus and group you would be attached to. Quite often, we would be taken to a large canteen and supplied with a Sunday dinner, then taken to the point of the march we would be based. Frequently, the march would start and end peaceably and many marches would take place with different causes and groups.

The trouble would start when two conflicting groups turned up at the same point. At that time WPC's were treated a little less equal and most times they kept us out of harm's way. It is fair to say that because men could take physical punches better than us they didn't put us in the front line. We were based in the vans and as the prisoners were put in, we were in charge of watching them and keeping them in the van. That is not to say that we didn't sometimes have to be a little firm with the prisoners. The women tended to be harder to handle, as will disclose in further chapters.

Some of the security jobs were a little more glamorous. One job, that was in central London, that required guarding the Jackson Five and The Osmond's. Both were staying at a largo London Hotel, the name of which eludes me, but the logistics of it was a nightmare. The Hotel was set on its own with a road surrounding it. The entrance to the hotel for the vehicles was at the rear and therefore, it required officers, mainly WPC's to be constantly vigilant on all four sides.

Fans had gathered from the early hours, cold and wet, they moved around, dodging vehicles just in order to try and see the balconies where they might get a glimpse of their idols. Unfortunately for us, Michael Jackson, who was a young boy at the time, frequently came out onto the balcony to waive and throw pictures out to the fans. This caused havoc as fans would feint, scream, become hysterical making it almost impossible to keep them out of the road.

A couple of the young girls had become so inconsolable they had collapsed and were almost finding it impossible to breath. We decided that we would take these two up to the suite for them to meet their idol. When we arrived at their room I knocked and their bodyguard came to the door. We explained the situation and within minutes the fan were introduced to the Jackson Five. I look back at that day and remember the door opening and seeing this new group. Little did I know that I was to become one of Michael Jackson's biggest fans and my son never forgave me for not having obtained his autograph?

The days guarding these two groups were fraught with danger. Not only did we have to contend with them running into the road, trying to get into the front entrance but at the rear of the hotel by the underground garage every time the groups entourage of limousines arrived or to with the members of the group we had to break our security chain to let them in. That signaled for the fans in the rear to rush forward, making it dangerous for them, by possibly falling under the wheels of the car.

At the entrance, the bodyguards would pull the artists out and push them into the limousines, whilst we held back the fans. After a couple of days, we perfected how to make it safer.

We would let the cars through then formed a body chain to hold back the fans. At that time, we were supplied with small shoulder bags in which we kept our notebooks and our torches. This is what we used to stave off the onslaught of manic fans. We would swing them in front of us making it impossible for them to reach us and break the chain, giving the artist's time to evacuate the cars.

The fans were ardent, they spent the whole three-four days in rain, and cold, and wind. Some of them with very little clothing on, waiting for someone to wave, arrive, or leave. A group of fans found where the Jackson's coach was which carried a lot of their costumes. They broke in and stole a large amount of their costumes and stage equipment as souvenirs before they were discovered and chased away. During the chase, one of the officers ran around the comer away from the main group of officers and when we realized where she had gone we followed only to find that a vicious group had been in wait for her and had attacked her and beaten her to the ground. When we found her she was obviously injured so an ambulance was called and she was taken to hospital.

We never did find the group responsible, but many of the fans that we had grown to know over the few days came up to see how she was and say how sorry they were that this had happened.

Home Office

A less traumatic and violent attachment, but equally interesting, was being based at the home office for short periods, escorting applicants that had failed to meet visa requirements and needed to be escorted back to the departure point, normally being the airport.

Sometimes it would be in reverse and we would be asked to interview applicants that wanted a visa or who were applying for their family to be given permission to come to the country. Many of the applicants that I dealt with lived in North London and were of West Indian descent or of Indian descent. Most of the West Indians had come to the country to work and get settled and had left their children with family in their home base, then they would each year apply for each of their children to come over. The Indian nationality mostly had British passports and therefore wasn't here legally, but their culture was very tight. Most of the wives did not speak English nor were they allowed out of the house or encouraged to become integrated. Their children would attend school but when at home their culture was followed vigorously. They would be applying for relative's and parents to be allowed to join them, too.

Each of them had different issues, but it was my job to ask all the relevant questions, and ensure that the application was genuine and met all the correct requirements.

One job came through to the station that required me to go to the home of a US citizen who was asking to extend his stay. I did not recognize the name on the paper but made an appointment by phone. But, when I arrived at the house, I was greeted by a bodyguard who told me that PJ Proby was resting in bed and couldn't be disturbed. It was about two pm in the afternoon and I informed him that my report had to be submitted at the end of that day as apparently his visa was out of date and if I didn't complete my report, then his stay might be cut short. As he was in the middle of tour then this brought a little urgency to the bodyguard. He was big and surly, and shuffled off. I waited in the lounge, which had medieval lighting hung from the center of the ceiling. Dark curtains were shut and the furniture in the room made it look dismal and dark. After about 20 minutes PJ Proby appeared in the doorway. He was dishevelled, and barely awake, and obviously not at all pleased to have been so rudely awakened just to come down and waste his time in talking to an officer. I kept the meeting as brief as possible, asking the necessary questions and making notes on the forms. He was asked to sign and without saying another word he turned and went back upstairs. The man was rude and arrogant and not someone that I had enjoyed meeting.

During my time in Borehamwood and Elstree, the experience was totally different. The film studios were almost next door to the station so quite often when we were on foot patrol we would pass by and take a few moments to watch the filming. We saw many artists performing and one of the scenes involved a pc and

WPC entering the shot. Whilst we were watching the director came up to us; and asked why we were not on set. At the same time another pair came round the corner and he realized his mistake. We should have jumped on set quickly and maybe we would have been on film and become stars.

Not long after, I had a report to file on a motor accident. Marty Feldman and his wife wanted to report a minor crash and I had to go and meet them on the set. The statement didn't take very long, but the difficulty was knowing which eye to look at when talking to Marty. If anyone knows the actor, they will remember that he had one eye that looked to the side and one to the front and he took turns in looking at you with different eyes. The question was which eye was looking at you, it was very unnerving. I decided that the most polite thing to do would be to look at the center of his forehead, that way whichever eye looked at me, then I had a gaze in the right direction.

It's a little disappointing sometimes when you see how an artist looks before the makeover. One of the stars that were off set was sitting her chair. She had rollers in her hair, no makeup, had a cigarette in her mouth and was not recognizable as the Elle Sommer that one saw as a glamorous artist that you saw on the screen. Some artists had a natural beauty, but so many would look so plain until the make-up artists performed their magic.

At my station, which is how I felt about it, of course I was just stationed there, I had initially to share with a WDC, a female officer in CID (Woman Detective Constable, Criminal Investigation Department). At that time, she was in the process of comprising and working on reports and evidence on the Kray Twins this was a fascinating time in London's crime history.

Kray Twins

The Kray twins were born in Hoxton, one of London's toughest East End neighborhoods. The area was crime-ridden and violent, with a long history of gang warfare. Hoodlums attained prestigious reputations, while regular working class folks descended into anonymity.

Ronnie and Reggie were identical twins, although Ronnie grew up heavier in build and slower in wit than his brother. Their mother, Violet, dominated the family, father Charles was a heavy-drinking. WWII military deserter. Both parents, while not exactly true criminals themselves, showed their sons by attitude and association that the police were oppressors of those daring enough to step outside the law. Their father's family was part Romany or "gypsy," this may have contributed to their sense of being outsider's in background-conscious English society.

Failure in Sports and the Military

The twins became successful amateur boxers as teenagers. They also joined a street gang and were arrested for the first time for administering a savage beating to another sixteen-year-old.

A short stint in the military resulted in dishonorable discharges for both, based on their repeated insubordination to officers and a tendency to go AWOL whenever they felt like it. At that point, the twins' boxing licenses were briefly revoked and then generously reinstated. However, the Krays decided that crime suited them much better than pugilism.

In 1954, at the age of 21, they founded the Kray gang. Reginald and Ronald Kray were notorious criminals whose obsession with assaulting others, encouraging each other to greater levels of violence, and extending their personal power and domination, culminated in a serious protection racket in London and a number of murders. Their blatant violence and unstable mental condition, particularly of Ronald Kray, led to intimidation of witnesses and the prospect of their escaping justice until they were arrested and convicted by the efforts of a special squad of detectives led by Detective Superintendent Leonard ("Nipper") Read.

The twins were born in 1933 and made their first appearance at the Old Bailey in 1950, where a case of assault was dismissed for lack of evidence. In 1952, they entered a period of National Service remarkable for their violence, serious trouble with the military authorities and periods in custody. After being released, they commenced a period of increasing control over criminals, pubs and clubs in the East End of London. On 5 November 1956, Ronald Kray was jailed for three years for assaulting Terence Martin in a gang related incident. He later became friends with Frank Mitchell in Wandsworth prison, and was diagnosed as suffering from paranoid schizophrenia. His violence worsened after his release.

In February 1960, Reginald Kray was imprisoned for 18 months for protection related threats. Whilst he was in prison, Peter Rachman, the head of a violent landlord operation, gave Ronald the *Esmeralda's Barn* nightclub in Knightsbridge served to increase the twins' influence in the West End, and with some "celebrities" and famous people, rather than East End criminals. They were assisted by a banker, Alan Cooper, who needed protection from the rival Richardson gang from South London.

Christmas 1965 marked a confrontation between the Krays and Richardson's at the *Astor* Club when a Richardson associate, George Cornell, referred to Ronald Kray as a "fat poof". A gang war followed, and a Kray ally, Richard Hart, was murdered at *Mr. Smith's* club in Cat ford on 8th March 1966. Ronald Kray took revenge by killing George Cornell in *The Blind Beggar* public house, Whitechapel Road. Intimidation prevented any witnesses from cooperating with police.

On 12th December 1965, the Krays assisted Frank "The Mad Axeman" Mitchell to escape from Dartmoor prison, but Mitchell became increasingly violent and unstable whilst staying in a flat in Barking Road. He disappeared and the Kray twins were later acquitted of his murder. The body was never recovered.

Ronald gave a gun and £100 to Jack "The Hat" McVitie with instructions to murder Leslie Payne and the promise of a further £400 when the murder had taken place. Payne remained alive, but it was Reginald who went to collect the £100. He was moved by McVitie's tale of sorrow and gave McVitie £50. This infuriated Ronald, and led to a stand-off between the Krays and McVitie, culminating in the Krays inviting him to a "party" where Reginald, egged on by Ronald, murdered him. McVitie's was another body not recovered.

The Krays tested Alan Cooper by suggesting that he carry out a murder, and Cooper, in turn, recruited Paul Elvey to do the work for him. Elvey was arrested, and Detective Superintendent Read's team interviewed him. Elvey confessed, and Cooper became implicated in three attempted murders. Through Cooper there would be evidence against the Krays.

The Kray twins were arrested on 9 May 1968 and once they were detained in police custody, witnesses slowly started to develop the confidence to give evidence of the truth to the police team. The trial lasted 39 days at the Old Bailey and the Kray twins were sentenced to life imprisonment, thereby removing from London a notorious criminal influence.

Long before joining the force I had socialized in the same areas that the Krays operated in and one of my acquaintances turned out to be the daughter of one of the Krays criminal victims.

This CID Office had also worked on the Moors Murder case. The Moors murders were carried out by Ian Brady and Myra Hindley between July 1963 and October 1965, in and around what is now Greater Manchester, England. The victims were five children aged between 10 and 17: Pauline Reade, John Kilbride, Keith Bennett, Lesley Ann Downey and Edward Evans at least four of whom were sexually assaulted. The murders are so named because two of the victims were discovered in graves dug on Saddleworth Moor; a third grave was discovered on the moor in 1987, over 20 years after Brady and Hindley's trial in 1966. The body of a fourth victim, Keith Bennett, is also suspected to be buried there, but as of 2010 it remains undiscovered.

The police were initially aware of only three killings, those of Edward Evans, Lesley Ann Downey, and John Kilbride. The investigation was reopened in 1985, after Brady was reported in the press as having confessed to the murders of Pauline Reade and Keith Bennett. Brady and Hindley were taken separately to Saddleworth Moor to assist the police in their search for the graves, both by then having confessed to the additional murders.

Described by the press as "the most evil woman in Britain". Hindley made several appeals against her life sentence, claiming she was a reformed woman and no longer a danger to society, but she was never released. She died in 2002, aged 60. Brady was declared criminally insane in 1985, since then, he has been confined in the high-security Ashworth Hospital. He has made it clear that he never wants to be released, and has repeatedly asked that he be allowed to die.

The murders, reported in almost every English-language newspaper in the world was the result of what Malcolm MacCulloch, professor of forensic psychiatry at Cardiff University, called a "concatenation of circumstances", which brought together a "young woman with a tough personality, taught to hand out and receive violence from an early age"

Having spent time listening to this officer, I felt that if I had stayed in the force then I would have probably transferred to CID as the work I would have found interesting and challenging.

Death Messages

One of the jobs that WPC's were quite often involved in would be escorting a PC (Police Offices) to deliver a death message. This part of our work was important, but very emotional as you knew that you would be delivering probably one of the worst messages that anyone would he wanting to receive.

I don't suppose there was one message I delivered that I don't still remember as if it was yesterday. At the time, I never knew the depth of grief that a parent would experience until I became one myself; nevertheless, it was a job that required strength and the ability to be a shoulder to cry on

The first one I had assigned to me was one that came in whilst on late turn, two to ten p.m. We had received information that there had been a motor vehicle accident involving a motor car and a motor bike. The bike had collided with the car, resulting in the driver of the bike and his passenger had been killed instantly. Neither one of the riders had been wearing a helmet and had head injuries been the cause of death.

Having received the address of one of the victims, the female, we headed off to deliver the news. At the door a young girl answered and opened the door. She was too young to know anything was wrong but normally it is accepted that if a WPC and PC arrive at your door, it is normally to deliver bad news. The mother came to the door and immediately knew something was wrong. The moment we asked if she had a daughter named— she had a sigh relief, believing that there could be no bad news relating to her daughter, as of course, she thought she was staying at a friend.

Once we told her that she had in fact gone out with her boyfriend on the back of his bike and been involved in a fatal crash her world fell apart. Her husband rushed to her side as did her two other daughters. They went into a daze, unwilling to believe we were telling the truth and insisting that we take them to the morgue where she was lying and waiting to be identified. All the way in the car they sat in the back asking very few questions.

Those that they did were in an effort to convince them that all this had been a terrible mistake.

The journey seemed endless, what can you say to a family who is about to see their first born lying on a marble slab. When we arrived at the hospital we escorted them to the morgue where the mother screamed out on seeing her young daughter. I never got used to the grief, that it was my job to deliver to a parent, how can you ever get used to inflicting pain even though it was not of your doing, it was in your hands to give out the news. We were taught to deliver it quickly, as dragging it out makes it worse. If it was a serious injury, opposed to death, then the quicker you tell them that no one is dead the better otherwise the imagination runs rife and can cause more grief than in necessary.

On one occasion that I shall always remember, I was working a night shift driving around in rural Borehamwood when we received a call from a farmer's wife. She had reported that her husband had gone out some time earlier to investigate some noises he had heard on the farm and had not returned. We drove to the Farm and drove back and forth along the lanes of the farm. It was a full moon and in the reflection of the moonlight in the middle of a field we could see a slight mound which seemed to be out of character to the rest of the area. We parked the vehicle and with our torches and moonlight walked slowly toward the shape. Lying face down was the figure of a male, crumpled over, it was obvious that he had been shot and appeared to be dead.

To avoid disturbing any evidence, we backed away and called for assistance and an ambulance. Why an ambulance? Well, until a medical person or coroner claims that they are dead, then we have to in these circumstance follow these guidelines, after all we could be mistaken and he might just need a doctor. We later learnt that he had disturbed a gang that was sitting in their car. He must have overboard or they thought he overheard, their plans, so not to take a chance, as he approached, they shot him.

Of course, the first thing I had to do was to inform the wife of what had happened. I drove to the farmhouse and as I walked in, she knew something was wrong. I sat her down and as best as I could do tell her that her husband and father of the children sleeping upstairs, had been shot and killed. I shall never forget the look on her face and the sobbing that then ensued for hours on end. I was her shoulder to cry on and I had to be strong, how I managed not to cry with her I will never know. The other officer had to go back to the station to make a report whilst I stayed with the family for the rest of the night.

When the morning finally arrived, a car arrived to pick me up, but not before I had to go upstairs to tell her young children as they woke up that their father was dead and that their whole life was about to change. The sound of those baby's cries were heart-breaking and if there is any justice in the world then the criminals that did this terrible thing should have those cries and sobs imprinted into their brain so that is what they hear night and day. But of course, that will never happen and I doubt if they ever gave it another thought, no regret or remorse for having ruined so many lives.

I left that house feeling totally drained and the moment I walked into my bedroom I broke down and cried for several hours. My husband who was already in bed was awoken to my cries and initially thought it was me that had been injured. No so at least not physically but mentally and emotionally probably. Now, officers that have to deal with traumatic events get counselling to help them cope. But back then, you just had to deal with it, which is why perhaps I have a photo vision of that night and of every traumatic event that took place which I can never forget.

Suicides

Many types of suicides are part of the incidents that officers are required to deal with, and can happen at any time in sometime the strangest circumstances.

When reporting a suicide, one of the first things you have to ascertain is whether it is in fact a suicide, accidental death or a suspicious death. All cases you attend are required to have the coroner attend and then he would decide on the evidence as to whether or not this was a straightforward case or whether it required CID intervention.

The coroner directs the investigation of deaths occurring within jurisdiction as required by law. His job involves supervising the activities of staff physicians, technicians, and investigators involved with conducting inquests, performing autopsies, conducting pathological and toxicological analyses.

He also investigates the circumstances of deaths in order to determine cause and fix responsibility for accidental, violent, or unexplained deaths, or contracts for such services with outside physicians, medical laboratories, and law enforcement agencies.

He testifies at inquests, hearings, and court trials also conferring with officials of public health and law enforcement agencies to coordinate interdepartmental activities.

He coordinates activities for disposition of unclaimed corpses and personal effects of deceased. He also is responsible for the activities of workers involved in preparing documents for permanent records and may assist relatives of deceased in negotiations concerning payment of insurance policies or burial benefits by providing information concerning circumstances of death.

Sometime, the coroner may be required by law or ordinance to have specified medical or legal training.

As you can see, the coroner has many avenues that he can follow and has to negotiate once a case has been reported to him.

Many times, I have a person who has taken their own life. On one occasion we were contacted by an elderly couple who had not heard from their son, so we went around to the house. When we pulled up his car was in the drive and the milk was on the doorstep and had been for about five days. We knocked and received no reply, and then we looked through the letterbox and could see why he was not answering the door. At the bottom of the stairs we could see a pair of feet dangling about three feet above the ground and at that point we know we had the right to gain entry. We broke the front door glass, reached in and opened the door only to find the young man hanging from a rope tied to the top of the banisters. It was obvious from the color of the man's skin and odor from the body that he had been dead for some time.

British Slang Definitions

Starkers—Naked	**Chips**—French Fries
Nosh—Food	**Give you a bell**—Call You
Ace—Cool	**Quid**—One Pound Sterling
Blighty—Britain	**Tenner**—A Ten-pound Note
Bangers—Sausage	**Fiver**—A Fiver-pound Note
Shambles—Mess	**Plastered**—Intoxicated
Chav—White Trash	**Stag night**—Bachelor Party
Tad—A little Bit	**Blimey**—My Goodness
Nicked—stolen	**Bee's knees**—Awesome
Tosh—nonsense	**Legless**—extremely drunk

In the kitchen was a letter addressed to his parents. The coroner was called and he pronounced the man was dead and opened the letter, which apparently apologized to his parents for having taken his own life. He had been diagnosed with cancer and the pain he was experiencing was so great that he could not bear it any longer and had decided to end it quickly. This was never a situation that was pleasant to deal with, and fortunately it was not one I had to deal with in regard to informing the parents.

I never really understood the reasons why most people take their own life, if it was a pain issue in a terminal case of disease then that I understand but so many were for reasons other than that. Loneliness, failure and grief were some of the reasons and I am sure that so many regretted their actions but had gone so far down the road that they were unable to turn back. No one was there to help. I often wondered when someone jumped from the roof and decided half way down that this was not such a good idea. That must be the worst feeling ever knowing that they didn't want to die now but had taken a course irreversible.

Sometimes we arrived in time and managed to get the person to the hospital in time to either stop the bleeding or reverse the reaction to the overdose...nearly not enough though.

CHAPTER TWELVE
SHOPLIFTING-THEFT

The basic definition of theft is defined in S.1(1) of the Act. The Act states that:

"A person shall be guilty of theft if he or she dishonestly appropriates property belonging to another with the intention of permanently depriving the other of it."

The law is quite specific, and it has no means of pre-judging anyone, all found to have committed an offence would be cautioned and arrested and charged. However, this is one offence that can be treated by a warning at the store by the manager if they decide not to prosecute.

There are many degrees by which this offence fits, all of which will explain.

Many times, officers would be called to a store to deal with someone found shoplifting. When someone was seen acting suspiciously in a store, then a store detective or member of staff would observe the person and watch exactly what she or he did whilst in the store. Many times the person would be seen to hide items under their clothing or put items in their own handbag.

Once the person has paid for her items, and left the store, without paying for the items she has placed in bags or places on her person, then they have actually committed the above offence. If they had realized that they had not paid for their goods before leaving the store, then no crime would have been committed. Once outside, then that is not the case. From there, one of the store's staff would then stop the person and ask them to come back into the store as they believed that they had goods on them that were not paid for.

Most times, they would deny the fact until we arrived and searched them and of course, they would then either make strong excuses or break down and apologize. In many cases, it was quite evident that this was theft and the store would ask to prosecute and we would then caution, arrest, and escort to the police station.

However, there are always the exceptions and the sad cases. There were the incidents where the person was very poor. Had no money on them and needed to steal food to survive, they would be very hard cases and quite often the store would not prosecute but also not allow them back in the store. Then there was the old and senile that would take items placing them in her own bag and leave the store. They would have money on them but had no recollection of having taken them without paying for them.

In most of those cases to the store would realize that there was no intent and that they were in need of help not prosecution and therefore would be escorted back home and perhaps a member of the family would be spoken to in order to try to avoid further incidents.

Of course, we then had the mentally ill patients from the nearby hospital who were allowed out for the day and would walk into the local town. Mostly the cases involving patients were easily dealt with by ringing the hospital and they would come and escort them back home. We had to be careful as sometimes if we were not aware of who was an inmate, we would have a situation that suddenly would erupt into violence and sometimes the sight of the police created the very thing we were trying to avoid.

One sad case I had to handle was one of a middle aged woman who had come to do her shopping as normal and had placed most deliberately a 2 pound bag of sugar into her own shopping bag. Once outside the shop she was approached and escorted back in. In this incident she had plenty of money in her purse and all her apologies went unheard as the store manager felt that in this instance she needed to be made an example of.

She was from a wealthy family and the stigma of a shoplifting charge brought against her with all the publicity it would also bring was too much for her to cope with. Her husband hired a lawyer to represent her in court, and of course, although I had to give evidence in the case I also felt for her. She was obviously very depressed and I suspected in need of some attention from her busy husband.

The case was in fact found in her favor and she was found not guilty by reason of not being in sound mind at the time of the offence. Although it was very obvious to those around that she needed help, the society circles she mixed in certainly would not find this social label very easy to wear.

I kept in touch with her after the case and it was quite evident that she was not dealing with this at all well. Several weeks later I received a call from her husband asking me to call round to her house as he could not contact his wife and she was supposed to be at home.

Another officer and I went around to the house to find it locked up, the milk left out, and the music playing inside. After checking for means of entry and knocking for some time on the door we felt that we need to gain entry to find out what was wrong. So, we broke a pain of glass in the kitchen to enable us to open the lock from the inside. We went into the house but could hear anything other than the radio from upstairs.

We went upstairs and found the wife lying unconscious on the bed with tablets by her side and a letter on the pillow. She was still breathing so we called an ambulance and she was taken to hospital where she was treated for an overdose. I think that this jotted the husband into the realization that his wife was indeed in need of help. She needed help from a specialist who could determine what she needed and give it to her. I believe she made a full recovery, but what a tragedy that would have been all over a 2-pound bag of sugar.

The next group would be the children, so many of them would treat it as a dare by other kids or just for something to do on the way home from school. Mostly, these were so young that they never made court. They would sit before a senior police officer and would be officially cautioned. However, if this was proved to be persistent, then they would go straight to juvenile court and dealt with there.

Some parents believed this to be unnecessary. They themselves had done it as children and saw no real problem with their behavior. Little did they realize that in some cases this was the beginning of a serious life of crime. If it had been treated as serious by the parents, as it could have been, then maybe their fate would have been changed.

There were many cases where a group from a school would take orders for the lifting session they planned. They would literally go shopping for items that others would order and then sell them to them cheaply, making a profit for themselves. Of course, these were the racketeers of tomorrow in the making, already finding an easy way to make a quick pound or two.

The least devious of the children just did it for the glory they received when returning to the school laden with their products, giving them out in an effort to gain friendships and favors.

Then we step up another level. To the parent who takes her child under the age of 10 years old to the store with her. The idea being to encourage the child is to take and hide items in hopes that they could get away with successful haul. Of course, if she was caught then she could claim it was the child who put the items in the other bag. Firstly, it would be hard to prove it was the mother, and secondly, if the child was below 10 years old, then they were below the age of prosecution as they were deemed too young to know they were doing wrong. Of course, the parent would know this so unless you actually caught the mother helping the child to conceal the items it was virtually impossible to prove. However, it didn't stop the store from banning them from the store. At least they wouldn't lose more goods.

Next step up: the professional teams. They would go window shopping, are normally in groups or pairs, enabling them to distract store assistant whilst they stole items and hid them on themselves. Putting on clothes under their coat or layering their clothes so that they could go out with four or five items on.

In the 60's & 70's they did not have the benefits of close circuit cameras and tags that set off alarms. It was left to the observance of staff and store detectives on duty to spot the criminals, and that was not always easy, as you will see.

One offender had thought this out very carefully and decided that she would try something a little different. When she arrived at the store, she had a large coat on and a large hat and appeared to be a very overweight woman. In truth, she was not at all. Under the coat she had padded herself out with towels and padding to make herself look large. So, she would take numerous items into the changing room, and in fact in those days, there was no assistant counting the items you took in, it was done on trust and you could take as many items as you wanted. She would load herself up with underwear, trouser, jumpers, blouses, and skirts. Once in the cubicle she would start to strip off all the padding, then layer by layer start re-dressing until she basically was filling up the coat again.

Of course, no one initially spotted anything was wrong, here was this big lady coming into the store and looking no different when leaving. Of course, sometimes she would stop off at the millinery department and whilst the assistant went to look for items she was requesting she would lift her hat and place a couple of terms under there.

She probably would have gone on for years doing this had not an observant store member noticed some towels stuffed in box and thought it a little strange. The next week, the towels appeared again. After three weeks of these appearing towels, they thought to keep an eye out a little more in the changing rooms. Then they were so amazed at what they then saw. Hundreds of expensive terms of clothing were being layered under the coat and over the time she had been visiting the store, many thousands of pounds of clothing had been stolen. Of course, this act of theft was punished by imprisonment.

Stores now have many security alarms and systems in place, the offences as I describe about are very unlikely to occur now. Probably, the majority of thefts happen in large grocery stores where it is not so easy to observe small items slipped into the pocket.

CHAPTER THIRTEEN
PROSTITUTION

Prostitution describes the offering and provision of sexual services for financial gain.

It is also referred to as the oldest profession, as it meets the natural urges humans in return for money and is often claimed to be as old as civilization itself.

In Great Britain (England, Wales, and Scotland) prostitution itself (the exchange of sexual services for money) is not illegal, but a number of related activities, including soliciting in a public place, curb crawling, owning or managing a brothel, pimping, and pandering are considered crimes.

The legal regulation of prostitution in Great Britain is set out in the Sexual Offenses Act of 1956 (repealed and amended in 2003), which reflects the findings of the Wolfenden Committee Investigation into prostitution and homosexuality that took place around that time.

One of the first places that come to mind if you mention prostitutes in London would be Soho. During the time I was in the service, this area was known as the area for ladies of the night, as well as the many services available in the many clubs, and strip tease bars, which were in nearly every doorway.

Originally, the area was farmland and was developed into a Royal Park by Henry VIII in 1536. In the late 17th Century, houses and buildings were developed for the upper class. It included St. Anne's Church, which to this day still stands where it was erected and remains a significant landmark.

Other churches are Church of our Lady of the Assumption, Saint Gregory, and St. Patrick's Church in Soho Square.

By the mid-19th century the aristocracy had mostly moved away when in 1854 a bad outbreak of Cholera hit the area.

In the 20th century, Soho had gained the reputation as a base for sex industry, together with a good night life and the headquarters for leading film companies. Since the 1980's, the area has undergone considerable gentrification and is now predominately a fashionable district with upmarket restaurants and media offices. There is only a small remnant of the sex industry and London's gay community in Old Compton Street, Soho.

During the years I served the Soho areas, it was full of the ladies in their doorways offering their services or hanging their legs out of windows trying to entice customers to pay them a visit.

It was quite amusing to see how the street changed as soon as a policeman came around the corner, legs disappeared, windows shut, doors shut. In those days a prostitute couldn't be arrested until she had received 3 cautions. The offer would take down her info and description, warn her and call it into A4. So, when she received the third caution, A4 would inform the officer he could take her in for processing which resulted in a court appearance and fine.

Some of the more clever of the ladies would use false names, dates of birth, colored wigs, and change of clothes so that when they were reported it didn't match the details from the last report. Some of them practiced their trade for some time before eventually getting arrested.

Prostitutes consisted of many types, from the 14-year-old looking for money to survive as she had run away from home, the drug addict looking for money for her next fix, and the professional who classed themselves as high class hookers.

Not only did they make a living, they made an excellent living. They weren't so at-risk walking on the street and didn't always have a pimp taking most of her income. These ladies marketed themselves through agencies or recommendations and quite often could afford a high end flat where to entertain her clients. They called themselves escorts or paid companions. Many had accountants to ensure they paid taxes on their high income making themselves as legal as they could.

I met one lady who was not only in the high end tax bracket, but it gave her an income that enabled her to have a luxury home in the country and put her child into a private school. Many of her clients were said to be lawyers, barristers, or surgeons. Some of which couldn't get satisfaction at home. In fact, she said that 80% of them didn't require sex, but other deviations. One like to be put into a diaper and nursed.

Twice a week he visited and paid her a very high fee for the service.

Another wanted her to dress as a schoolgirl and be his mistress, scolding him about his behavior and hitting him with a whip as punishment.

One gentleman had a fetish for women lingerie, and once dressed fully in his attire would want to talk about fashion and paint her nails, again no sex involved.

Of course, these ladies were few and far between, and the majority of the street ladies risked the dangers that still exist today from men that pose as a client with more sadistic and sick fantasies that he wants to fulfil. Curb crawlers would drive by and stop to see what the charges would be for a certain service and if the lady decided she was happy to provide it, she would get in the car and go somewhere quiet to perform the paid act.

Some of these ladies had a pimp who would want to protect them, because if they got beaten up or hurt, they couldn't work, so quite often he would be in the area watching his girls. If the prostitute worked from an apartment, he would be close at hand watching.

Peter William Sutcliffe (born 2 June 1946) was commonly referred to as the Yorkshire Ripper. He is now known as Peter William Coonan, changing to his mother's maiden name. He is an English Serial killer, convicted in 1981 for murdering 13 women and attacking several others. He preyed on prostitutes because of their vulnerability.

When he was caught, and eventually convicted, he was placed in a prison on the Isle of Wight, but claimed that he was mentally sick and was eventually moved to Broadmoor Hospital, a prison for the criminally insane.

He was attacked by several prisoners over the years and has lost one eye and partially blind in the other, slashes on his face and attempts to strangle him. He appealed his sentence in 2010, but it was dismissed. They felt he was deemed not to be insane but to be put back into a regular prison, never to be released. Not many in the prison system tolerate offenders with a history like his.

During his reign, there was a tremendous fear among prostitutes, and many were scared to go back on to the street. However, most of them had no other means of support, and therefore, put themselves back at risk. Police presence was very evident on the streets, but unfortunately many didn't take precautions and would go off with strangers, which is why he managed to kill so many.

Unfortunately, in one of the cases he murdered a young girl on her way home, not a sinner, as he considered all the others.

Amsterdam had a more liberal view to the business of prostitution. It took them off of the streets and placed them into rooms in the Red Light District. It is legally monitored, they have regular health checks, and customers look at them behind the window and knock on the window to find out services offered.

They have a light system and the older the lady, the redder the light as apparently it hides age effects. It takes the women off the street and of course takes a lot of the risks away. I've always thought that if the profession is to continue, then it's better to have it controlled from every aspect.

TRAMPS & FLEAS

The two of these together was common, just by the nature of the beast, as the conditions in which most tramps live in does not afford them the ability to wash or keep up cleanliness to any acceptable standard. I learned early in my career that there are many variants, and not all tramps are in that position of their own free will, but some believe that to sleep under the stars and be free of responsibility is the only way to live.

Some of the characters that crossed my path did so, not because of any crime, but because they were considered a public nuisance. One woman was spotted regularly visiting a public convenience, but because it was at set times there was a question as to what she was doing in there. When I checked it out, I found this woman was using the toilets to wash her feet in them to try and remove the lice, and then she would wash her face in the same water.

When I questioned her about where she lived, she told me she and her partner lived under a local bridge close by. I walked back with her to find her partner who was asleep under a pile of newspapers. As we approached, he stood up to welcome us to the home they had made, which consisted of plastic bags to keep out the rain and a few sticks of broken crates, and a few bags or rags which I guessed were their clothing. There was a pot brewing a disgusting looking liquid which was balanced on top of some burning wood. They told me that this was their evening meal made up of scraps found in the bins of restaurants and anything else they found in the bins.

For everything I saw, I felt sorry for these two souls, and they were so sweet and gentle, even to the point of offering me some of their evening meal that made me want to throw up but it made me realize that for all they didn't have they were prepared to share it.

This was like a scene from Oliver Twist and no way that anyone should be living in the 21st century. These two continued to tell me how they had lost their jobs, got into debt, and borrowed against the house from moneylenders. You can guess the end result, they were evicted, possessions lost to the lenders.

Homeless overnight and nowhere to live, which meant they couldn't get a job without an address and couldn't afford to rent without a job so they were pretty much screwed.

I had a decision to make a choice, I could have walked away, but I had to do something! With the right contacts, you can call on social services to help find them emergency accommodation, with food and ability to wash and get re-clothed. Their level of intelligence was low, and I was pretty sure that this couple would count as a part of the protected persons who were at risk in these situations.

After a few calls, I spoke with a social security officer who agree and a police van arrived to pick them up with their possessions to take them to the shelter. Once there, they were met by social services, who after enquiries, found them council housing and both a small part time job which at least gave them a new start so they could be safe and in a dry place.

By standards, that was a success story and I can only hope that the system kept working to their advantage. Many other groups living under the stars chose to do so and refused help to go live under a roof. Many had dogs as companions, and they slept together for warmth. On one occasion, we had a local tramp who was born into a wealthy family, he had everything he wanted in life, but at the age of 24 he told us he was jilted in love and from that point he decided that he wanted nothing from his present life and if he couldn't have her he wanted nothing. He bought a mobile home and four dogs, and that was his life, sleeping outside sometimes and just walking the streets. His family sent him a small amount each month to stay away and that's how he lived. He never did any harm to anyone or made a nuisance to anyone. He was one of the local characters. He died of old age, lonely, and without knowledge of his family. What a waste of a life, but what a love he must have felt to have thrown his life away.

Sometimes though, they can present unseen problems. One female I was called to do a search on was going to be charged under the Vagrancy Act, and before being locked in a cell she had to be strip searched to ensure there was nothing on her that could do any damage to herself or an officer.

As she took off her clothes, the unseen companions buried in her clothing started looking for another home and began hopping around. Lice stay on dirty skin, but fleas aren't proud and will go anywhere it is warm and cozy! All of her clothes were removed and put in a bag to be burnt ASAP. She was then given other clothes and placed in a cell.

Once I finished my shift, and my first thought was to get home and shower as quickly as possible. With exception of my skirt and jacket, everything was placed in the laundry and washed as they appeared to have a few visitors… the uniform looked fine. Or so I thought… The next morning having washed my hair, and redressed with clean shirts, I was the source of amusement for the entire early shift at the station, who were informed of last night's guest in the cells. Whilst telling the story, I started to scratch a little, then a little more. The officers closest me started to scratch. Then within 30 minutes, everyone was itching. We thought it was all in the minds, talking about it made everyone scratch, but then we saw some friends jumping on my shoulder. At this time, the duty sergeant bundled me into the back of a van and took me down to the local mortuary where they had a delousing department.

That was the last place I wanted to go. I was told to strip off and they would put me on a slab and scrub me down…oh no that wasn't going to happen. I wasn't sure if this was a set up by the comedians at the station which would be in keeping with their sense of humor. I never did find that out, but I agreed to a compromise. I would shower with the delousing shampoo and they could take my full uniform for delousing. I managed to escape without being on the dead persons slab… even now just talking about it makes my skin crawl.

The next time a vagrant came in for an inspection. I tried to make sure I was occupied…once bitten twice shy (literally bitten.)

CHAPTER FOURTEEN
Escorts

Missing children

Escorting was another of our duties that we would get assigned to. They could come up at regular intervals and there was a vast difference in the types of escorting.

It always involved women or children, but the escort could be vastly different and required vigilance at all times.

Runaways quite often ended up in London because we all know that the streets of London are "paved with gold." Unfortunately, lots of children thinking that getting to London would totally change their life, would be very disappointed. It certainly would change their life, but not necessarily for the better. As with most runaways, they do it totally unprepared, no money, no food and very little clothing. So, when they arrive, they tend to wander around in amusement arcades, in places where it is warm, dry and out of the elements. Because so many of these places are open for long periods of time, some of them would find a place in the corner to cut up and get some sleep whilst they could.

Piccadilly was a favorite source for runaways, plenty of arcades and very close to Soho which has always been a point of fascination for those brought up in rural England.

Of course, because this is where many can be found. It also attracts less desirables looking for these runaways. They are perfect for their needs. Some are pedophiles looking for innocent children to supply their depraved needs and they approach them as friends offering them food and somewhere to live. When a young child is desperate cold and hungry they see nothing more than a way out, not realizing that they are going further into a black hole they might never come out of.

The others groups preying on these children are pimps looking for fresh meal to supply their customers with Children, both young girls and boys are in great demand for pornography, and prostitution. They offer large sums of money to get them hooked, and then once into the system they are kept in prestigious houses, living well with offers of a constant income giving them a lifestyle they perhaps have never experienced. Of course, pimps and others take a pretty good living off of these children. To add to the need of these children they put a mother figure in charge of them to give them the emotional stability and at times. If the children get a little difficult, they introduce them to the delights of drugs. Once they get dependent on them then there is nothing they won't do for another fix and then they have total control.

The damage done to these children can often be irreparable. Once found, then the job of society is to try to get them back to normality. If these children are found soon enough, then we can try to get them back home. As long as there are no situations at home then quite often the children are pleased to be taken back. They don't often admit that, but the moment that you open that front door, and Mum and Dad are waiting there for a tearful reunion, it becomes very clear that they are pleased to be home.

The children not found in time need for more help than just being reamed home. Some wood hospital treatment for drug issues, sexual diseases, and physical abuse. Some survive and manage to recuperate, but some unfortunately decide that the life they are living is high earning and easy, so they decide they want to stay in it. Even if you find them, they run away time and time again until society gives up on them or just can't find them again.

Prisoners/ warrants

Those not deemed a flight risk or a danger to take on public transport would be taken back to their hometown and delivered to the local station or court that had issued the warrant. Quite office someone would be picked up in the streets for behaving in a manner that was suspicions or were involved in a crime. When a check was run and it turned up that there was a warrant for their arrest, then they would be taken into the local station and an escort would be ordered to take them back.

On one such occasion, I was asked to go on an escort to the Midlands, Manchester. In fact, I would be going by train with another officer to take a young 17-year-old girl back, wanted on warrant. Because we are going to other constabularies, and the nature of the escort, then we would be on this occasion in plain clothes. We picked her up at a police station in central London, collected our travel warrants, and then headed off to the stain station. Once we got onto the platform, we stocked up on refreshments and waited for the train.

She was in handcuffs and we took it in turn to be handcuffed to her as discretely as possible.

There is nothing as unnerving for a member of the public to be sitting on a train opposite someone in handcuffs. So, once on the train we decided to take off the cuffs. There was nowhere she could go whilst the train was moving. She would sit next to the window with one of us opposite and one to the side. Even when she wanted to use the bathroom, we would have to check out the toilet to make sure she couldn't get out of the window, even on a moving train some might consider the risk worth it.

Then, we would need to keep her in view, either with a foot in the door or go it with her. You need to remember that a toilet has the ability for a prisoner access to a weapon that she could use on her or on one of the officers. Most bathrooms have a miner and if smashed then a slice of glass is a great instrument for slashing wrists or slashing one of us.

One might think that our security measures might be a little extreme, and probably 99 out of a hundred the prisoner might never do anything but just one could cost us our life or the prisoners. So, the journey to Manchester was a long and tiring one, both of us would have to be on guard for every minute. To lose a prisoner would be a nightmare and would end up with severe punishment and certainly writing reports for weeks.

The particular prisoner was not very talkative and certainly was not too happy about being returned to her hometown to answer charges, which would inevitably end up in a prison sentence.

Eventually, we arrived in wet dismal Manchester. We in the south always joked that in the northern part of the UK it rained constantly, and guess what it was raining.

It was raining heavily, and we left the train with a handcuffed prisoner and met the police escort that was waiting to take us to the central station. Once at the station, then the prisoner was officially handed over, and with the look on her face wasn't expecting any gratitude for a comfortable journey home.

The only good thing that resulted in escorts like this was that they would put as up in a good hotel, pay for a good meal so that we could relax and get some rest after a long tiring day. It is surprising how tired escorts make you; I think it is because you have to be vigilant the whole time. At least now we could get some sleep and get ready for the same journey back the next day.

Home Office

These escorts came up occasionally. We would be called to the Home office in Central London and report to the main reception. Then there would be a briefing as to the circumstances of the case and told how we should treat the escort with regards to the height of security. The majority of them were immigrants who were in the country illegally and they wanted to ensure that they were escorted back to their point of departure. These people were quite often just ordinary people who had wanted to live in Britain, either because they felt they would have a better life or because they wanted to join family and friends already here. Some would be from the Eastern Block, which in the 60's had no freedom of movement, and of course the freedom that a citizen receives in the UK must have been very appealing to someone who lived under communistic rule.

Holloway

These were probably the least popular, they certainly were for me. I remember the first time I was given an escort to the infamous Holloway Prison for Women. Not a pleasant experience.

Originally constructed by the city of London and opened in 1852 as a mixed prison, it became all female in 1902. This was one of the most depressing of places you would ever want to see. The first time went here I decided that this would be the best deterrent for anyone; it certainly would be one for me

The dark stone that the exterior of the prison showed to outsiders was entered through two large wooden doors. As you stood in front of them it took you back to another century, times when people were put into prison for stealing a loaf of bread to feed a starving family. Now the prison housed murderers and criminals from all walks of life, all now being women. I hated the place. The moment you walked in to the large courtyard there were gates and stairs and a whole miss mash of badly designed corridors.

On one occasion when we entered the building inmates stopped doing what they were doing to stare and call out obscenities. They observed the female we were bringing in to begin her sentence and straightaway you could see that they were summing her up to see which side of the fence she would be sitting. I am not talking about a garden one either. The life of a female prison split into two groups. Those that wanted to keep to the heterosexual way of life, some being married with children, then there were those that decided that if men were being kept away from them by society they would turn to their own sex for gratification. Some of the women came into the prisoner as heterosexual; but left as either bi-sexual or a lesbian. Not all women were given the choice. If someone of a strong nature and high up on the chain of prison decided she wanted a new "bitch" then if you were the chosen one, then you really didn't have much choice in the matter. To this day, I still shudder when I remember those hours spent escorting to that prison.

On this particular day it was hot, and the male officer and I stayed close together, neither of us being very comfortable in the environment that we found ourselves in. As we entered, we handed over our prisoner, who herself look shaken a little after taking in the initial impression of the prison. I am sure that there must have been some part of her at this exact moment wishing that she could turn back time.

We were both in shirtsleeve order, which meant we were without a jacket and had our short sleeves rolled up. We were totally the center of attention, which neither of us relished. The prisoners from the top balcony were calling out obscenities to me and to the male officer with me. He whispered in my car that if this group got out then he wasn't sure who would come off the worse hiss or me. Sexually, we would both be attacked.

We were escorted to the canteen so that we could get lunch. Of course, the prisoners ate in a different canteen. The food was not had, and we ate up as quickly as possible, as neither of us wanted to stay longer than necessary. We went back to the office, collected our paperwork needed to take back to the court and headed out to our car

As we started the car up to leave, a female office came up to me, leaned in through the window, stroked my arm and whispered in my car that perhaps I would like to meet up with her later…my goodness, even the officers, or at least some of them, were joining the other side.

I told the officer to put his foot down and get us the hell out of there. As soon as those gates opened will were out of there quicker than a rabbit out of the trap. I have no problem with people's choice of sexuality but when officers approach me in that manner it was totally inappropriate and quite unpleasant. I have to say that this is one of the escorts that I tried to avoid if I could. It would be at the bottom of my list for sure.

Mental Hospitals

My station in Borehamwood also had several mental institutions in the district, some of them very large so needless to say we got a lot of enquiries and escorts. Not all the patients were on a criminal placement order that had them in a secure wing but they were required to stay there. They were under an order for a period of time either to assess or for treatment. So quite often they would go missing and we would have to go find them and bring them back. Some would be found quite quickly, some would get further away using public transport, and some unfortunately would take their own life or would die in the colder weather from exposure, having got lost and unable to find help.

I learnt early in my career that mental health was something that I had no leaning toward. Those suffering from this disease, which they could not help, could be so unpredictable. Most criminals have logic, weak spots, and are able to be persuaded or reasoned with.

Even if you are offering a deal for their sentence they understood and were able to respond under normal circumstances.

However, these patients we were dealing with were so scary, one minute they would be talking normally, then the next screaming or kicking and ranting, and then they would change back as quickly as they started. There would be this glazed look that came over their eyes and their behavior would suddenly change without warning. They would be so strong that it made it almost impossible to restrain them. Quite often they would have to have a straitjacket put on them that would stop them hurting themselves and others around them. A method long since gone, I just didn't like dealing with situations that had no control over, and I was not trained in dealing with mental instabilities.

When we returned a patient to the home, not only was it unnerving when you went inside it was also so sad. To see so many young people that were in these institutions and probably would be in there for many of their youthful years. As we entered, we would be taken through the corridors, each one being locked behind us as we went through to the next section. So many locks, so many patients walking around you, drugged and in a daze. Once someone had escaped then they put him or her in a more secure unit. It was always a relief to leave these units. I thanked my lucky starts that I was never struck down with mental illness that would have necessitated a stay in a home.

So, in truth, that was another type of escort I didn't volunteer for unless I had no choice.

I am sure that with medical breakthroughs many of these homes now are closed as they can treat patients in society with drugs and new therapies.

My mother-in-law worked in a large mental institution in Wiltshire and had done so for many years. She had seen such a change in the system. She would tell me that in 30's and 40's, young women were committed to the home by family members for having given themselves to a man before marriage and ended up pregnant. They would be committed and not just for a short period, but for the rest of their life. The child when born would be adopted.

Those in control would be persuaded by family members that the woman needed help to protect themselves from their self. Of course, it was because the family did not want the disgrace that the pregnancy brought on the family. The wealthy families quite often donated to the home to ensure that no one would be the wiser. I just wonder how many of these unfortunate women in those years ended up in this situation.

Many of those women lived their whole life being punished for one mistake and never entered back into society. They were so institutionalized that, when in the 70 and 80's they tried to rectify these situations and release these women who had had no mental illness.

Of course, it was impossible to release them, they were now almost mentally incapable of living in the outside world and that is where they would stay, never seeing their child again or in fact anyone that had meant anything in their life. My mother in law would regale me with stories of these women whose only crime was to fall in love with the wrong man.

Of course, it wasn't just getting pregnant that ended them up in the mental home, there were women put in there for just beginning a relationship that the family deemed unsuitable and didn't approve of. Of course, this was normally in the upper class of society. It happened in the lower classes, but they would be thrown out and made to find their own way, either with the man or in a workhouse. The route aforementioned was definitely the route for those that had money and could bribe the institution to hold the women. After all, it was assumed that if a lady of means was involved with someone who was considered undesirable and refused to stop the relationship she must have been mad. That was sufficient to convince the authorities that this woman needed to be confined. I shudder when I think of how that poor woman must have felt. The family not only shunned her but also committed her to an institution for the rest of her life in poor and pathetic conditions. I am sure that she probably did end up mentally ill. To someone from the upper class, this would have been a traumatic experience, which I am sure very few, survived.

A famous UK singer tells stories of how in her youth she fell in love with a young officer whom her parents did not approve of. They decided to avoid disgrace to the family and for her own protection she was committed to an Institution. During the second World War, she found a way to escape otherwise her whole life would have been a different story.

Initially, these institutes were called Lunatic Asylums, and if you read throughout history these housed anyone in society that were suffering from anything that didn't conform or fit into society. Apparently 10% of inmates would die within the first three months of being placed into the Asylum, probably from inadequate medical help or inappropriate treatment. Some of the patients not only acted differently, they look differently. Some of them having been kept in attics for years, the family not wishing to show them to the world for want of the shame that they would feel. Eventually, they would resettle them in homes that relinquished them from any other responsibility.

She told me stories of padded cells, straightjackets, electrical shock treatments and much more. Most of which I had dealt with and seen when escorting prisoners who were placed in the Psychiatric care. Thankfully things have changed for the better.

She had one patient who was special. Her name was Elsie Leach and in 1914 she had a breakdown. Her husband placed her in the institute with instructions she should be there for the rest of her life. She was always telling the nurses that her son was a famous actor. No one believed her but in truth she was in fact the mother of Cary Giant, who, at 11 years old, had been told by his father his mother had died. At the age of 30 years old, he discovered that his mother, after suffering an episode of "mania" had been placed in the Bristol Lunatic Asylum. He was instrumental in obtaining her release and looked after her for the rest of her life.

It is a great example that sometimes people are telling the truth about a situation and because they are deemed insane no one believes them. Thankfully, in this case, it had a happy ending.

CHAPTER FIFTEEN
ALDERSHOT HAMPSHIRE CONSTABULARY.

In the 1960's the housing market was booming, which didn't help young couples trying to buy a house in Central London. I married a fellow Police Officer in 1970, and after living in Police Married Quarters for a while, decided that we should look to buy our first home. Prices were at a premium and they were rising at a thousand pounds a week. We basically missed the boat and couldn't keep up with the price increase.

My husband was from Wiltshire and I was from London so we had to decide where we could afford to live. My husband didn't want to Police in an area where he had many friends and relatives living so the next best choice was Hampshire constabulary. We applied as a couple and had grand thoughts of being given a home beat in the country with a little police house and having the responsibility of running our own little village. Well, the reality was that they wanted to put us in a flat in Portsmouth Town on the south coast.

We had no problem with the town, but with an Alsatian dog as our family pet, the flat wouldn't work and as no houses were then available in the area the next posting offered was one in Aldershot. We agreed to the posting and in the beginning of 1972 we moved to our new house and jobs.

Little did we know that we were about to move into a town that was about to be the subject of one of the worst attacks on British Soil.

The Aldershot Bombing occurred on 22 February 1972 in Aldershot, Hampshire, just three weeks after Bloody Sunday. It was the official Irish Republican Army's largest attack in Britain during the troubles, and one of the last major actions of their armed campaign before their ceasefire in June of that year.

Their target was the headquarters of the Parachute Regiment, which had been heavily involved in the Bloody Sunday shootings in Derry. A Ford Cortina with a large bomb hidden inside was left in the base car park, deliberately positioned outside the officer's mess.

The time-release bomb exploded suddenly on the morning, and the blast destroyed the officer's mess and wrecked several nearby army office buildings in an explosion which could be heard over a mile away.

The intention was to target soldiers who it turned out were not present, as the regiment itself was stationed abroad and most staff officers were in their offices, not in the mess. Nonetheless, seven people were killed, including an elderly gardener, five kitchen staff just leaving the premises and Father Gerard Weston, a Roman Catholic army chaplain who had just parked behind the car bomb. The explosion also wounded nineteen people. Authorities were shocked and concerned by this first major attack in Britain, and poor security at many bases was tightened up in an effort to prevent a repeat of the attack.

We arrived just after the attack and of course being the main station in the town we worked very closely with the Army on security in and out of the barracks.

The name Aldershot may have derived from "Alder", indicating that it was a wet, boggy place. Aldershot, Alreshete, dates back to an Anglo- Saxon settlement. Aldershot was referred to in the Doomsday Book of 1086.

In 1854, at the time of the Crimean War, the heath land around Aldershot was established as an army base with Aldershot at its center. This establishment led to a rapid expansion of Aldershot's population going from 875 in 1851, to an excess of 16,000 by 1861 (including about 9,000 from the military). The town continued to grow, reaching a peak in the 1950s.

Queen Victoria was a regular visitor to Aldershot and a Royal pavilion was erected for her use. For her Jubilee Review in 1887, 60,000 troops lined up in the Long Valley. They stretched from the Basingstoke Canal to Caesar's Camp. Royalty and VIPs from all over Europe and the British Empire attended the event.

A substantial rebuilding of the barracks was carried out between 1961 and 1969. The town was designated an experimental site by the government and various new building technologies were employed with mixed success

The BBC reports that Aldershot is currently receiving £12 billion as part of a huge regeneration project, and in December 2007 it was named one of UK's most popular places to live. However, when we first arrived in the town, it was far from the perfect place to live.

Aldershot is known as the home of the British Army, and it really was. There was a pub on every corner and when the Army was in town, we all knew about it as you will see in the following pages.

Before we could start work in the station, we had to attend a familiarization in Winchester at Police Headquarters to make sure we knew about the local laws. In the Metropolitan Police Force there were laws that were specific to that Force Which Constabularies outside the Metropolitan area did not have the benefit from.

So, we spent time back in the classroom learning the local laws and procedures that in truth varied considerably in certain aspects. It was obvious that officers in Hampshire were more restricted in their ability to make decisions without the permission or knowledge of a senior officer.

That probably was the most difficult thing to deal with; how much of what we had done in the past was not to be allowed in the constabularies.

Firstly, in the court system we were used to presenting small cases in the magistrates' court where now a solicitor handled everything.

One of the powers we had was to arrest someone as a suspect. In other words, if an officer saw someone acting suspiciously and hadn't actually committed a crime but was acting in a manner that lead the officer to believe he was about to then he could be arrested and brought in for questioning. It was a great preventative' in stopping a crime before it had happened.

Of course, some officers in the past that had transferred had not realized that they had lost that power of arrest and had used it, which meant that had caused some serious issues for Hants. So this was one point that was put over time and time again to ensure we knew this was a power of arrest that we were unable to use in Hampshire.

Many of the differences in the two forces appeared over the next few months when we were actually working in the station. I was greatly surprised as how different two forces could be. Women in the Metropolitan Force had a much wider range of duties and responsibilities, whereas in the constabulary, at least this one, I found that we were expected to keep within a much smaller range of duties, which of course, was very frustrating and gave us less variety to be involved with. Of course, the different departments were much smaller, and therefore, rarely needed officers to stand in or assist as they had their own female officers attached permanently to the department.

For my part, one of the most noticeable changes in duties was that they had set departments which used WPC's for undercover work opposed to the Met that pulled in WC's from division. So mainly now, my duties were dealing with Children, young persons, shoplifters and all dealings that involved women.

Now, all work involving undercover work, drugs, similar serious crimes, they used women within their department. The downside to that was that their face was well known and didn't give them the same ability to hide their identity. In the Met they would pick women officers that looked most unlikely to be an officer opposed to the 'A' typical career officer who sometimes stood out in civilian clothes as an officer. However, that was the policy and any officer transferring in was going to have to abide by the rules if going to fit in. For some reason because I came from the London area they treated us with a little trepidation. I think they felt that London, being the center of sin and debauchery, that all offices must be crooked and on the take. I was amazed at how many fellow officers had a totally wrong opinion of officers in London. I know that many officers in London believed that all constabulary officers were a little un-street wise so why should there not be a reverse incorrect opinion from this end as well.

I think over the years there was a certain amount of distrust and resentment between London and the constabularies which probably was a result from times when all serious crimes in the suburbs required an officer from London to come down and investigate. That probably made the rural officers feel a little superfluous and the London officers very superior hence this situation, which even to this day, has remained.

My husband was based in Farnborough and I was based in Aldershot, which was either side of our home so the travel was now reduced to a minimum, which suited us both.

From day one, I had to rebuild the trust between the CID and myself and also fellow male officers. It takes a long time for both groups to accept a WPC, as most seemed to believe that we would be better at home looking after kids and that this was a male domain. Many officers would give me a hard time until they know that I was prepared to work hard, not shied away from unpleasant tasks and could hold my own in a dangerous situation. I totally understand where they were coming from after all if you came upon a murder victim and the female officer with you fainted, threw up or burst into tears not only did it make it look unprofessional, it also put more responsibility onto the other male officer.

Of course, a new WPC also had the same challenge of introducing herself to the wives. This particular station also had a club house upstairs above the station so that gave us the opportunity of meeting everyone after the late shift and on occasion the WPC's took turn in helping behind the bar so that we had the opportunity to get to know a lot of the wives. The job was hard enough without having any complications from family disputes. Some wives were very jealous of their husband working alone with a policewoman especially on night duty and every time there was any gossip or news reports of an inappropriate tryst then we had to repair damage done to our reputation by someone miles away

Now, although I was totally in favor of female rights and the ability to do the same job as my male counterpart, it is a physical fact that a women officer cannot take a punch or blow to the body as well as a man can, but equally there are duties that only women could do such as dealing with women prisoners, and young children.

Of course, I am very much typecasting us as women officers and that is probably not too accurate. I can remember many female officers that were built like brick shithouses and could throw and take a punch better than a lot of men I know. Also, there are some men, fathers in particular that can be better with crying children than a WPC who has a dislike and lack of experience of children. So, there are always exceptions to the rule and that is probably one of the things that Police College never prepares you for.

Nothing is always as it seems.

CHAPTER SIXTEEN
Death of a Niece

I am still amazed at how after all the years that have passed, I can still recall so accurately events around traumatic cases. Officers now when dealing murders and serious crimes are given therapy and help to avoid having any emotional scarring. Not so in the past, an officer was expected to deal with anything that they were involved with and there was never any suggestion that the events you dealt with would have any long-term emotional effects.

Then why, after over 30 years, I can close my eyes and visualize the circumstances, the areas, the faces and the bodies so clearly? Why can I still remember those faces of pain when gave them the bad news? I doubt that my life has been ruined by dealing with such events but what emotional damage might have been done by carrying this around for so long I have no idea.

On this particular day, I was on a normal day shift in Aldershot and working between my office and the front office. A man walked into the office to report his niece was missing

The sergeant on duty asked me to interview the man and take a statement. I led him into the interview room, and sat him down, and took some information from him and went to get the paperwork I needed. From the moment he sat down in the room, I had a feeling something wasn't right. If you were to ask me what it was that I was uncomfortable with, then I couldn't have told you, just a feeling

He had apparently taken her out with him to the military grounds where there were bushes of Blackberries growing. When they arrived they realized they hadn't bought a bag with them for putting them in, so he sent her back home to get one. She never returned back, and he went back home to look for her but she had not returned house.

After years in the job, when I dealt with men that have a history in child offences then for whatever reason I used to get a feeling I cannot explain but it was never wrong. I went straight into our local information office, where an officer was responsible for gathering information on local crime and offenders so that we had at our fingertips the ability to run a quick check to tell us if we needed to do any further investigations. As soon as I looked this man's details, a story was unfolding before my eyes making it more and more likely that this had more to it than you'd first expect.

The moment I read his history of abuse and offences, I knew something was wrong. I knew that we would probably be looking for a body, and not a lost child. I immediately told the duty officer and called CID to come in with me to do the interview. Once I had discussed with them the circumstances he had reported, my findings in his criminal record then it was decided that CID would take over and continue with the interview.

Whilst he was interviewed, he was adamant that he had never seen her again and he pretended to be so upset, crying and saying that he felt so guilty that he had let her go off on her own.

I was sent round to the home where he lived with his wife. She was a lot older than him and on speaking to her, she admitted that they had been having some troubles in the bedroom. That morning, they had had a really bad argument and he had gone off angry. He had gone round to her sister's house to see if he could take the niece to pick blackberries.

The more I listened to the history, the more I was convinced that we were dealing with a serious crime. On returning to the station and reporting my findings it was decided to get a search party out with as many officers and police dogs as possible. Our hope was that we would find her lost in the woods, but each of us knew what might be found.

We went to the area that she was last seen and everyone started covering the area. After about two hours, a whistle was blown. Everyone stopped what they were doing, whether it was speaking or searching. The whole area full of officers went deathly silent, everyone knew what that meant. The whistle meant that a body had been found. We all headed back, and in the distance, I could see the tape being drawn around an area where a small lifeless body lay crumpled and still.

On the way back to the station, no-one spoke, many cried. These are one of the times that I hadn't wanted to be right; I was hoping my gut feeling would be proved wrong. Once back at the station, the CID confronted him with the information and he broke down and cried denying any knowledge of the death. It took sometime before he admitted having killed the child.

I then had the unenviable job of having to go back to the home to give them the news. Two sisters whose life would never be the same, one had lost her child and one whose husband took her life and now she would lose her husband to a life imprisonment. How does anyone deal with that? I have no idea how a family can get over that. The wife had no knowledge of her husband's past record, and if she had, then most likely she wouldn't have married him and certainly would not have exposed her niece to his control.

I have long learnt that in this job "What If", are some of the biggest two words there are. What if I had said no, what if I had not done that, what if I had checked. It is the two words that you could put to many scenarios and so many use it after the event.

CHAPTER SEVENTEEN
Cruelty

From my time in the force, as with everyone else who has served you will find everyone will have a "pet beef."

It could be drugs, it could be domestic violence, it could be the politics in the force.

Some might not have a particular thing that gets them upset, but I pretty much know that my "beef" was cruelty.

It comes in many shapes and forms, mental cruelty, domestic violence, cruelty to children, cruelty to animals.

All these have always upset me, but in varying degrees.

Domestic violence is one crime that happens all too often and in many walks of life. One thinks it happens in lower levels of society where the man comes home drunk and hits the wife about. You are right that is common and often the neighbors are aware and do nothing or the wife is too scared to do anything. It would be joked about at the pub, "he had one too many and went back and gave his missus a good hiding."

However, as time has gone on, more and more of this violence has crept up into the upper classes, the neighbors now are distances away and don't hear it, and a lot of the children are in boarding school or don't see or hear it. And of course, the wife has money to get it covered up by a beautician so it's not noticed. Some violence done by lawyers, doctors, politicians, people that can't use the excuse that stresses of no money was the cause.

The one thing that is common, is that most women believe it is their fault...they upset him, they said the wrong thing, he was tired, he didn't mean to punch my face or break my arm, he really loves me.

Most will refuse to have them charged and if they do by the morning they will withdraw the complaint.

Overnight, the husband has sobered up and said his sorry and it won't happen again...until it does.

The other husband who can't blame it on drink will profess his love and that he was stressed as work and she should know better than to say or do what she did. Flowers, jewellery and sweet words… and they believe it...until the next time.

Each time it is the same, each time the injuries are worse, but each time she believes it was her fault.

Mostly because they loved their husband, they can't believe this will continue, they feel guilty that it must be them doing something wrong. The only thing wrong they do is stay in that environment because eventually unless help is obtained, not only will serious damage will ensue there is the likelihood of death.

Where children are present, then they are emotionally damaged and if they don't see their father punished, then they grow up believing it is normal and it runs the risk of another generation either accepting getting Beaten or being the beater.

In some instances, I have managed to get the wife into a mother and child refuge and obtained a court order for the father not to see or visit and then and only then does the wife have the time to speak to other beaten wives but time to realize that not of it was her fault and that she deserves better than being a punch bag.

A lot is unseen, and sometimes it is mental cruelty and oppressive behavior. I have to admit, it is most frustrating when you sit in a hospital ward with a woman has had her face beaten to a pulp has broken arms, fractured ribs, and numerous unspeakable injuries and refuse to charge their partner with serious assault, knowing it will happen again, and again.

Child Cruelty

This is a different kettle of fish. These aren't adults that can demand it stop and walk out, these are poor defenceless young children who can only look up at their abusers and ask why.

I have had babies in their cribs with cigarette burns all over their body, as the father put them out on him. One little one had teething issues and you know that it is painful and they cry. This father decided he was tired of the crying so he put the baby in a bath of boiling water. Of course, that really stopped the crying! Or the mother who didn't like the latest baby. The house was immaculate and the two oldest children were well taken care of but a neighbor heard crying from a back bedroom constantly and knew she had had a third child but never saw it.

When we investigated, we found the back bedroom locked and when entered, we found a small half-starved child lying in a crib, covered in feces and urine without clothes on and had his anus passage pushed outside of his body through straining. He was covered with sores and infection and this baby had been allowed to suffer at the hands of the mother and the father felt that the mother knew how to deal with a difficult boy.... he was eight weeks old.

This child survived, thankfully, but if the neighbor hadn't called no one would have known. I can't tell you how angry this made me feel then, and to this day.

We as a society have a duty to protect those that cannot protect themselves. I dealt with case after case of child abuse and neglect, which made me realize how bad the situation is and how much goes unseen, unheard and unpunished. I think the worst case that heard about was when a group of drug traffickers were looking at ways to increase their ability to smuggle drugs into the country unseen. The following was how they did it, but I warn you it is not pleasant.

They employed, in a third world country, a group of woman and paid them each a sum to get pregnant. Once born, they took the babies, killed the child, and then emptied their abdomens, filling it with drugs. They then stitched them back up, and paid the mothers to travel to the UK with their infants. No one checked on the babies as they appeared to be sleeping, until a flight was delayed a long time. By the time they flew, the babies had changed color and were giving off an odor, they then discovered this terrible group of traffickers and murderers and what they had been doing.

I have to say, that left many of us speechless, that humans can reach that level of depravity is beyond anything I would think is possible.

Cruelty to Animals

Another inexcusable act that defies reason. To harm defenceless animals and torture them or use them for bait for dog fighting was another cause for heartache. Those poor animals even after all they went through would still wag their tail when someone was kind to them. How they tolerated being in the presence of human beings, I still don't understand. I would expect them to tear and bite us and yet the first sign of love they are shown they give it back. Cruelty to both animals and children, I suppose, angered me the most, as they are two groups that have no choice other than to suffer at the hands of those that should know better.

In my own personal view, and I emphasize that, I truly feel that if you mistreat a child or an animal, then you should never be allowed to have charge, care or control over one ever again. You can draw your own conclusions about your own thoughts on the subject.

CHAPTER EIGTHEEN
Met v Hants

I now started to realize the difference between the Metropolitan Force and the Hants Constabulary. I didn't think that there would be much of a difference but there certainly was, From the attitude to senior officers, the responsibilities that women officers were restricted to and the general attitude towards procedures.

I had a soft spot in my heart for the Metropolitan Police Force as that is where I started and had spent several years with many fine officers. I resented the attitude that existed in the Constabulary that all officers in the Metropolitan Police must be corrupted. They viewed transfers from the London Force with suspicion and mistrust, something I never really understood.

The London inner and outer areas had vast areas of serious crimes, racism, prostitution, corruption, and crimes related to overcrowding and poor housing. The inner divisions covered areas that attracted large amounts of tourist which of course were easy pickings for bag snatching and petty thieves. It also had the reputation of having streets paved with gold, which resulted in being a magnet for those young runaways from the outer counties to head towards to find their fortune, or at least a better life. Of course, that all being untrue meant that there was a large % of children arriving into London were at risk, with nowhere to stay, and a totally unrealistic opinion of what they would find when they arrived into London.

Here was one of the big differences. The larger towns in a constabulary did not have the same draw that London did and although they had their own issues, everything was on a much smaller scale. Even criminals had been known to drive up to London from their own county to rob or break into houses in high end districts, then return back to their hometown.

Resentment over the years had built up, and having been on both sides of the coin. I can to a certain extent understand it. When Robert Peel created the Police Force his "Peelers" were the leaders in the formation of the force we now see today. So, because London is the capital of England, everything was based there. Even though local rural areas formed their own force, whenever big crimes occurred officers from London were sent for. I am sure that in the 1800's the London officers made the rural officers made them feel inadequate and unable to deal with their own problems. That would have caused ill feeling when officers had to relinquish their files and officers to the visiting officers, who probably took over the whole investigation using the local officers for menial tasks. Of course, when they solved the crimes then that probably fuelled the resentment and over the years it grew. Even to this day, that underlying suspicion of the London Police is still there.

On the opposite side, the London Officers felt that the country officers were inexperienced and slightly stupid, believing wrongly that a strong rural accent was a sign of poor education and let the local officer know that. So, it understandable how this deep seated feelings going back 100's of years, still have some work to do, in order to make the systems totally compatible.

I clearly remember when the Metropolitan Police were called in to assist Hants constabulary in the protection of witnesses and security during the IRA trial in Winchester. I was in the Met then and was greeted by rural officers who looked us with suspicion, and still, the Met officers who commented that they were there to help out the "yokels".

Once I transferred to the Hants constabulary, then I saw it from the other side, and it was interesting to hear the views of the constabulary. When an officer came down one day on an escort the comments were "There's a smart arse from the Met coming down, just keep an eye on him." I had to smile, just what had to be done to break this never-ending circle? We were all officers trained in law enforcement, just had different challenges.

Women Officers

This area of policing was vastly different. In the Metropolitan Police, having been through the integration period, where women were then legally accepted into the force and were able to demand that they be treated equally with the ability of being able to apply for higher ranks and different departments, including mounted branch, dog handler, serious crime squads, and many more. I had grown used to being used by undercover departments on aid for various assignments that required plain clothes and undercover jobs. No-one would recognize that any of us were officers and our job was as an officer, and not as a woman police officer.

It was a complete shock when got pushed into the "women officer" slot. In the constabulary we were now still looking after children and females and shoplifters. They didn't use us as aid to any of the serious crime units and used those that were already in that department, even though their face was well known and perhaps looked like a police officer, even in civvies. I had to smile that my first undercover job was with officers that just put a jacket over their uniform, kept the police shoes on and their blue shirt, both of which stood out like a sore thumb! I was beginning to understand why the Metropolitan Police did not give much credence to their ability to fight crime with the same expertise. Of course, the moment any officer from the Met dared to make a suggestion of how to improve something, they would be told quite clearly that "Those London ways won't work down here, we don't need any of their help thanks, we can do things quite well without their suggestions or help" So you can see why I still felt that conflict.

HAMPSHIRE CONSTABULARY

Certificate of Service

THIS IS TO CERTIFY that

Woman Police Constable Maureen BRIDGES

served in... Metropolitan Police ...from 23.9.68 to 26.11.72

and served in the Hampshire Constabulary from 27.11.72 to 14.3.75

Reason for leaving the Force... Resigned

Conduct... Exemplary

Chief Constable of Hampshire

CHIEF CONSTABLE'S OFFICE,
WINCHESTER.

Date... 14th March, 1975.

This Certificate is without erasure of any kind

[see over]

CHAPTER NINETEEN
Charges

I suppose at the time of joining the Metropolitan Police I had no idea that I was stepping into a part of history. The Women Police Department gracefully became part of the Force and I was now a police officer who happened to be female. Big changes started to take effect, which began with our duties, which were now not specialized.

During the first few months on division a policewoman had to attend "specialist" courses so they knew the laws appertaining to children & young persons. They also needed to know all of the rules and regulations that needed to be followed together with all the other departments inside, and outside of the force that you would need to be competent in contacting.

For instance, at any time that a child was found in a circumstances that required protection then a place of safety would be needed. This required contact with Social Services who would then, after being informed about the case, would find a place in a foster home or children's home until the case was resolved, at which time it was decided if the child was to go home or permanently placed in a home.

So, the practice was that whenever women or children were involved, they would call a WPC and we would take over the case. We had the knowledge and expertise so it made it the most efficient way of dealing with these situations. Once we became part of the force and were totally integrated, then this was one of the things lost. They never called a WPC, and so at the start the PC's dealt with the cases themselves. Initially, it was havoc as none of them had our training or knowledge of the laws covering this field so it had to be a quick learning for all of them and of course if a WPC happened to be around they would try to get some help from them if they were not involved in another job.

Equality brought some great advantages, but it also brought about changes that were not necessarily good, that is in my opinion and I am sure there would those that disagreed.

For instance, when there were riots or demonstrations, we were kept at a distance, in the vans, and as eyes for watching the prisoners. Once we became equal, then that changed and WPC's were now in the front line, arm to arm with their fellow officers. Now some female officers were built to take a punch and were built to deal with the street violence they would encounter, but the majority were not, and this is where I saw the problems. Woman, albeit can be fit and strong, they have areas in the body that are more susceptible to damage if hit.

Integration, to me, was inevitable and it was the right thing to do, However, women are built differently and we both bring different qualities to the policing table, equally important but just different. There were many policewomen that wanted to be equal in many of the same fields as men and so it changed in my mind not for the better. We were able to be dog handlers, mounted branch, CID Special Branch, various other departments. The fact of it is, if you are equal you are equal and there were no exceptions, so men had to deal with jobs they didn't like and so did women. The advantage the men had was that if women or children were involved, especially with body searching, then they would call a matron on duty, opposed to calling for a policewoman.

Another change that emphasized this was TV programs involving policewoman. They always showed the WPC running around after the men making them cups of tea and coffee, which of course, annoyed me immensely. That happened, but nowhere as much as the programs would have you believe and it always demeaned policewomen in my mind, but I notice now that those same TV shows have police women out there in the thick of it. Of course, in the early years of my service there were many men that felt that women should be at home having children, and making tea should be their duty. The shows have become more realistic and reflect a more accurate position that the female officer now works in.

The job I knew and loved had changed. When I discovered in 1975 that I was expecting my first child. I worked up until my sixth month, and then went on maternity leave. We were allowed to take six months off on maternity, then we had to decide to either come back full time or resign. Unlike today when you can come back and work around the family, then it was all or nothing. I always felt that so much training was wasted, and reluctantly I handed in my notice to spend my time looking after my new baby.

Many of my friends stayed in the job long after I left, some of them making it a career without taking time off for a family. They would tell me in detail how the job had drastically changed and that I wouldn't recognize the job any more, and not all the changes were good.

There was a great family feel in the stations and we all knew each other and each other's families. In a lot of the stations, we had a bar which was our social club, which after a late shift or an early shift meant we could bring in the families and socialize with each other. Soon, the clubs were to be shut down, shifts changed so that the closeness between each shift became less and less. They became strangers to each other only meeting on shift at work. It seemed like they wanted less of the family environment at the station and less friendships amongst the officers. Was this a good thing? Well time will tell, personally I have my own view on it, and perhaps I was becoming like the old officers I was first stationed with.

We all used to laugh at the old timers, on their last

legs of 25 or 30 years career, when they would say to us "In the good old days, it was so much better." We all used to roll our eyes, believing that we were in the best times, now I found myself doing exactly the same. I nearly pinched myself when talking to a policewoman one day telling her that things were so much better in the 70's. She rolled her eyes and I knew exactly what she was thinking. As a policewoman we had our own chief superintendent and high-ranking officers who were responsible for our hiring, training, and well-being. We knew everyone by name, as they did. I was amazed when I spoke to this new policewoman or other female officers and they knew very few outside of the station.

It now was so different. The Woman Police Association still exists today in the form of a club you have a membership to, with magazines, yearly meetings and monthly outings. Each issue brings names of officers I remember from years back that have passed away. The sad thing is, we all hold special memories of those times gone by, of a time of great change and excitement within the force. However, once those officers have all gone, then there will be no one to remember how it was.

I hope that this book has given those who read it a small insight into what it was like to have been a policewoman in the late 60's. I thoroughly enjoyed my years in the force and am grateful for all those friends I made, some of which are now longer not with us. I hear about those passing and so many of those in my training year have died, either from accident, disease or just age.

For those of you out there who know or knew me, I hope that this book will bring back some memories both sad and happy and that anyone considering a career in the force will take the bull by the horns and go for it. Whether mine was a better time in the force, those before me or those after me, who can say, it is a fact that each generation will benefit from different things.

My seven years in the police force changed me as a person, and how I perceived life and those around me. I think can say it made me a stronger person, able to deal with tragedy and emergency situations better than I had before. I am far more aware of the other side of life that exists, the darker side that most people will never see or have to deal with. I have seen things that I would not wish other people to see, I have dealt with people that were at the bottom of society, but I also dealt with normal people who had had situations to deal with, whether it be death, tragedy, crime or just a bad situation. I would like to think that I made a mark somewhere, and if just one person out there was grateful for my help and appreciated that what I did made a difference, then my time spent in this career would not have been wasted.

Time changes people, and things and people change time. Be one of those people. I would like to think that I am.

RESEARCH REFERENCES

For more information on the Moors Murder

"Hindley: I wish I'd been hanged." BBC News. 29 Feb 2000 http://news.bbc.co.uk/2/hi/uk news/661139.stm

For more information on the Kray Twins

"History > Famous Cases > The Krays". Metropolitan Police Service Archived from the original on 11 July 2016.

https://web.archive.org/web/20160711214824/

http://content.met.police.uk/Article/The-Krays/1400015485453

"Kray Twins" 12 Dec 1965

ABOUT THE AUTHOR

After having various professions including secretary and ground hostess, Maureen Coonrod joined the British Police Force. A female police officer is called a WPC (woman police constable) several nicknames were used i.c W Plonker and Bobby Dazzler albeit not commonly used. She served in the late 1960s to mid 1970s before leaving the force with an exemplary service record. Since leaving the force, she's ran a hotel worked as a language school agent, and worked in a managerial position for a district sales company. In 2004, she immigrated to the United States from the United Kingdom and became a US citizen.

Currently Maureen works as a realtor in Florida. On her free time, reading crime fiction & thrillers, traveling, listening to country music, and spending time with her dog, Reba, named after country legend Reba McEntire.